W9-AXR-074

Teaching Women's History Through Literature

STANDARDS-BASED LESSON PLANS FOR GRADES K-12

KAY A. CHICK

NCSS
Bulletin 107

National Council for the Social Studies

8555 Sixteenth Street • Suite 500 • Silver Spring, Maryland 20910

www.**socialstudies**.org

Editorial staff on this publication: Michael Simpson, Chi Yang
Design/Production: Cowan Creative, www.cowancreative.com

Library of Congress Control Number: 2008927024
ISBN: 978-0-87986-101-0

Printed in the United States of America

5 4 3 2 1

Table of Contents

I dedicate this book to my parents, Monzell and Jeanie Anglin, for their continued love and support.
Many thanks go to Bill, Tyler, and Tim, for their encouragement and good humor.
They know how to make me smile, even on my bleakest days.

Why Teach Social Studies?

Social studies is an integration of the social sciences and humanities. When students learn about issues and problems in history, political science, geography, sociology, and psychology, they become better decision makers and better citizens in our democracy.[1] Although educating students for citizenship appears to be a lofty and worthwhile goal, many schools no longer devote adequate time to the teaching of social studies, especially in the elementary grades.[2] The Council for Basic Education has determined there have been decreases in social studies instruction in grades K-5 since 2000, especially in schools with a high percentage of minority students.[3]

In most elementary schools, instructional priority is given to language arts and mathematics, with the argument that students cannot take part in civic responsibilities unless they have learned basic skills.[4] In addition, the No Child Left Behind Act mandates the evaluation of students in grades three through eight in reading, math, and science.[5] Social studies is not included in these assessments, and teachers prioritize their school day according to those subjects for which they are accountable. These dynamics result in students entering middle school without knowledge of social studies concepts.[6]

When social studies is taught, many teachers rely on textbooks, which provide a concise view of history and social studies concepts. However, students often see social studies textbooks as boring and without relevance. One educator describes social studies textbooks as "deadly dull" and suggests that "history is a story and textbooks eliminate the story."[7]

Why Teach History?

History is an integral part of effective social studies instruction. Learning our nation's history is critical to preparing students for involvement in democratic practices and the responsibilities of citizenship. As with social studies, history classrooms often rely on textbook-based approaches, and in such cases, memorization of names, dates, and places become standard fare. Schools that are overly reliant on textbooks frequently have concerns about meeting state and local standards, and lose focus on best practices.[8]

When traditional approaches to teaching history are utilized, students acquire a descriptive accounting of historical events, but few skills in historical thinking, problem solving, or interpreting the past.[9] If students are to think critically about history, they must consider questions such as, Whose history is this?, What perspectives or viewpoints might be missing?, and, Are parts of history silenced and why? History textbooks may present a narrow perspective, told from the viewpoint of the "winners," while the history of women, minorities, and the poor may be silenced.[10]

Why Teach Women's History?

Studies from the 1960s to the 1990s revealed that women were essentially invisible in history textbooks. Textbooks simply omitted topics that focused on the issues and contributions of women.[11] An evaluation of a 1992 edition of one frequently adopted history text found that only 3% of the book's content was devoted to women.[12] Textbook content was written from a male perspective, and women's contributions were not integrated within the text, but were treated as sidebar notes.[13] This lack of female representation is of great concern. If students do not understand the role of women in history, they will misunderstand the organization of our society.[14]

Recent studies suggest some progress has been made toward gender balance. An evaluation of 18 high school American history textbooks revealed there were 1,335 females in those texts and 12,382 males. The researchers also discovered there were more women in illustrations, with 616 named women and 3,505 identified men.[15] The 2005 editions of one elementary, one middle school, and one high school United States history textbook were also assessed for gender representation. In both text content and illustrations, all three texts contained significantly more males than females. However, in comparison to earlier studies, women are being portrayed in greater numbers.[16]

In 2004, the American Historical Association stipulated that American history textbooks must be balanced with respect to race, class, and gender.[17] However, they failed to define the word "balance." Considering that males have had a significant impact on the historical record, it may not be realistic to anticipate a 50/50 split in gender representation. However, teachers must consider the limitations of any history text and integrate resources such as diaries, videos, primary documents, simulations, and children's literature, to supplement the teaching of women's history.

Integrating History and the Language Arts

With time constraints a major consideration in curricular decisions made in K-6 classrooms, history is often forgotten or set aside for special occasions such as Black History Month or President's Day. Many children in the younger grades know little, if anything, about history, while students in the intermediate grades may have limited, but often skewed, knowledge of topics such as war, Indians, and famous people.[18] Students who enter middle school with limited exposure to historical concepts may find themselves at a great disadvantage.

Many teachers are considering curriculum integration as a way to emphasize literacy skills and teach social studies and history concepts at the same time. Curriculum integration is designed to incorporate information, perspectives, and instructional strategies from various disciplines.[19] Studies suggest that an integrated curriculum fosters student engagement[20] and attitudes towards school,[21] and increases the relevance and level of challenge of the curriculum.[22] Students who participate in an integrated curriculum with highly skilled teachers perform academically at levels equal to, or higher than, students in traditional classrooms.[23]

History and language arts can be easily integrated with the help of children's literature. Trade books are an excellent resource for presenting historical concepts and events to students in the primary, intermediate, middle school, and high school grades. They bring drama to historical events and their impact on people, humanizing history in ways that textbooks cannot. They allow students to connect with characters, real or fictionalized, supporting their interest and engagement. In addition, both historical fiction and biographies encourage students to become curious about various time periods, consider difficult or sensitive events, and become involved in discussions of diversity and social justice. Students are able to learn about the past within the context of authentic, meaningful, and engaging text.[24]

In the elementary grades, picture books and chapter books can be used to teach language arts skills such as word identification, reading comprehension, narrative and expository writing, speaking, listening, viewing, and visually representing. In the middle school and high school grades, historical novels and biographies can be integrated into reading and English classes. Teachers can emphasize reading to learn, while also encouraging students to refine their writing and speaking skills. The middle school and high school grades also offer opportunities for reading, English, and history teachers to team teach or participate in integrated curricular planning.

Trade book selections are critical to the teaching of history. Books should be selected that are factually accurate, free of stereotyping, representative of diversity, and respectful of cultural differences. They should also include illustrations that precisely reflect the historical period. Above all, trade books must be appealing to students and include content that is developmentally appropriate.[25] They can be read individually, with a buddy, or aloud to the class, depending on students' reading levels, the objectives for the lesson, and the extension activities that follow.

How an Integrated Curriculum can Support Social Studies Standards

Extension lessons and activities should be planned in accordance with lesson objectives for both history and the language arts. Many school districts create curriculum guidelines for history and social studies using *Expectations of Excellence: Curriculum Standards for Social Studies.*[26] These national social studies standards detail what students should be taught and methods for instruction and assessment in the areas of civics and government, economics, geography, and history. The standards are organized into ten themes and provide a framework for the design of social studies programs in grades kindergarten through twelve.

The social studies standards are based on the position statement of National Council for the Social Studies.[27] This document outlines the principles of teaching and learning that must be in place for social studies programs to be considered excellent. The principles state that social studies teaching and learning must be meaningful, value-based, challenging, active, and integrative. The position statement recommends the integration of topics, skills, and teaching and learning across the curriculum. Therefore, the standards promote integrated learning opportunities and the formation of interdisciplinary courses.

The second theme in the social studies standards is ❷ TIME, CONTINUITY, AND CHANGE.* This theme indicates that social studies programs should help students to understand the ways human beings view themselves in and over time. Performance expectations differ in early, middle, and high school grades, but the teaching of this theme encourages students to

---

*   The NCSS Standards references are to the ten themes of the NCSS social studies standards. For convenience, all ten themes are listed on the inside flap of the back cover of this book.

compare and contrast stories of people and events in the past, use various sources for reconstructing the past, use facts from the past to inform current decision making, describe selected historical periods, and develop attitudes such as empathy and skepticism regarding the people and events in history.

Many of the classroom examples included in the standards represent integrated curriculum. For example, an eighth grade class studying the American Revolution is reading *Johnny Tremain* and *My Brother Sam is Dead*.[28] Students analyze both novels in literature discussion groups from multiple perspectives, and then develop a list of criteria for assessing a contemporary issue from different perspectives. Each group prepares a news story and an editorial about their issue and gets feedback and assistance with editing from their peers. Students get opportunities to learn historical perspective, while also improving their writing skills.

Fostering Girls' and Boys' Interest in Women's History

When integrating children's and young adult literature into the teaching of women's history, teachers must first consider gender differences in the area of reading. Boys and girls do differ in reading achievement, reading preferences, and time spent in literacy activities. Boys consistently score lower on tests of reading achievement and are more likely to be considered reluctant readers.[29] Studies show that children have preference for same-gender protagonists, although females are more likely than males to cross gender lines and read books with male characters.[30] Girls tend to enjoy fiction, with stories that describe relationships between people. Boys prefer books about sports, adventure, science fiction, war, history, and cartoons, and seem to be more affected by popular culture. They are drawn to non-fiction, graphic novels, magazines, newspapers, and biographies.[31]

There are numerous reasons for these gender differences, but some educators believe the ways schools are designed and the instructional strategies they use seem to favor girls. Boys need to be active, favoring a hands-on approach to learning. In the area of literacy, it is not that boys don't read, but they tend to read materials that are not readily available in schools, such as sports cards and magazines.[32] It's not that boys don't like to write, it's that they like to write stories about violence, war, and alien invasions, topics which are not always valued in classrooms. These gender differences are firmly in place in the elementary grades and continue to affect literacy practices in adolescence.[33]

How then, do teachers get both girls and boys interested in women's history? Both girls and boys may be attracted to exciting stories about the adventures and accomplishments of women, given that they have heard very little about the deeds and endeavors of female historical figures. However, if some boys are reluctant to venture into a book with a female on the cover, teachers may need strategies to spark their interest.

Teachers can begin by focusing on genre, given that boys typically enjoy history and biographies. Selecting a high-adventure biography or historical non-fiction book and reading it aloud, even to middle school students, sets the stage for future selections. Building background and fostering curiosity by discussing the setting, historical events, and time period, may be enough to entice males to give a book a chance. Involving students in the reading of a wide choice of historical novels, with both male and female main characters, helps students realize similarities among characters. Other strategies that can be used to broaden students' reading preferences include author studies, abundance in book choices, and school-wide reading programs that demonstrate that adult male role models can be avid readers of women's historical fiction and non-fiction.

To maintain students' interest, extension activities must be active and hands-on, with considerable variety. Planning activities that incorporate all of the six language arts (reading, writing, listening, speaking, viewing, and visually representing) encourages students to demonstrate their knowledge and problem solving abilities in a multitude of ways. Allowing students to incorporate their interests as they explore characters, events, and time periods in historical fiction and biography, encourages creativity while maintaining their enthusiasm. For example, boys may choose to write stories or participate in skits that bring adventure, suspense, and danger to the lives of historical female characters.

About This Bulletin

This bulletin is designed to provide teachers with literature and extension activities for children and young adults, to support the teaching of women's history. The bulletin is divided into grade-level chapters — teaching women's history in the primary grades, the intermediate grades, the middle school grades, and the high school grades. The final chapter offers thoughts on teaching women's history through literature and recommendations to make the transition to literature-based history instruction less of a challenge. The extension activities take an interdisciplinary approach by integrating women's history and the language arts through children's literature. With this approach, elementary, middle, and high school teachers can teach women's history while emphasizing high-priority literacy skills within the time constraints of the classroom.

The literature highlighted in each chapter was first selected because of its high literary quality. Many of the books were award winners, representing the Coretta Scott King Award, the Robert F. Sibert Medal, the Parents' Choice Award, and the Michael L. Printz Award for Excellence in Young Adult Literature. Other selections were chosen as Notable Social Studies Trade Books for Young People by National Council for the Social Studies or were on the *New York Times* Bestseller List.

All of the book selections present positive female role models. Each book invites readers to become engrossed in the story and identify with characters, as well as learn valuable historical information. The characters take risks, display a range of emotions, confront important historical dilemmas, and encounter ethical, social, and moral issues. In addition, the girls and women represented are authentic to their historical time periods. The authors represented have not distorted history or culture in order to create capable female role models.

Although it was impossible to include all of the famous women in American history, care was taken to represent those women who have made a significant contribution to our nation's past. These representations include famous women, such as Eleanor Roosevelt and Rosa Parks, as well as women who may be relatively unknown in history classrooms, such as Alice Ramsey and Daisy Bates.

The literature selected contains developmentally appropriate content and illustrations. A book's theme and readability were considered to ensure that each selection was appropriate for its intended grade level, keeping in mind that many books are suitable for multiple age and grade levels. The books represent diversity in genre, ethnicity, and time period, and are factually accurate and free of stereotyping. They represent themes which are considered to be historically significant. The literature includes historical fiction, biographies, and poetry, and consists of picture books and chapter books. Based on the diversity of reading abilities and interests in the high school grades, the collection at this level includes a mix of young adult literature and adult selections.

Keeping teacher accountability in mind, each book and extension activity was chosen for its alignment with standards and performance expectations from *Expectations of Excellence: Curriculum Standards for Social Studies*. This document acted as a framework and guide as books were selected to correspond with one or more of the ten themes.

Although the books are divided into primary, intermediate, middle school, and high school levels, teachers should make book selections based on the needs of their students. Most classrooms have great diversity in reading levels and language arts skills, so, for example, some of the middle school literature might be appropriate for the intermediate grades. Please note that many picture books have been incorporated into intermediate grade activities. It is a misconception that picture books are only suitable for primary grade children. There are many picture books, in fact, whose content is not appropriate for young children. For example, *Ebony Sea*, the story of the Ebo people who decided to drown themselves rather than face a life of slavery, is a picture book that is better suited for the intermediate or even middle school grades.[34]

References

1. National Council for the Social Studies, *Expectations of Excellence: Curriculum Standards for Social Studies* (Washington, DC: National Council for the Social Studies, 1994).

2. Elizabeth R. Hinde, "Revisiting Curriculum Integration: A Fresh Look at an Old Idea," *The Social Studies* 96 (2005): 105-112; Yali Zhao and John D. Hoge, "What Elementary Students and Teachers Say about Social Studies," *The Social Studies* 96 (2005): 216-222.

3. Council for Basic Education, *Academic Atrophy: The Condition of the Liberal Arts in America's Public Schools* (Washington, DC: Council for Basic Education, 2004).

4. T. Turner, *Essentials of Elementary Social Studies*, 2nd ed. (Boston, Allyn and Bacon, 1999); P. Vanfossen, "Reading and math take so much of the time… An overview of social studies instruction in elementary classrooms in Indiana." Paper presented at the National Council for the Social Studies Annual Conference, Chicago, IL (2003).

5. Greg Toppo, "Reform Causes Subject Shift; Schools Leave Behind Social Studies to Satisfy Bush Education Program," *USA Today*, March 9, 2004: D8.

6. Hinde, 105.

7. Dennis Denenberg, "Teaching with Heroes," *Millersville Review*, available at http://muweb.millersville.edu/~heroes/mureview.html.

8. Zhao and Hoge, 216.

9. Gary Fertig, "Teaching Elementary Students How to Interpret the Past," *The Social Studies* 96 (2005): 2-7.

10. Steven Wolk, "Teaching for Critical Literacy in Social Studies," *The Social Studies* (2003): 101.

11. David Sadker and Myra Sadker, *Failing at Fairness: How Schools Cheat Girls* (New York: Schribners, 1994); M. Tetreault, "Integrating Women's History: The Case of United States History High School Textbooks," *The History Teacher* 19 (1986): 211-261; J. Trecker, "Women in U. S. History High School Textbooks," *Social Education* 35 (1971): 249-260.

12. Sadker and Sadker.

13. L. Reese, "Report on Gender Equity and History Texts at the Secondary School Level," *Transformations* 5 (1994): 62.

14. J. Baker, "Women's History," *American Heritage* 55 (2004): 66-67.

15. R. Clark, J. Allard and T. Mahoney, "How Much is the Sky? Women in American High School History Textbooks from the 1960s, 1980s, and 1990s," *Social Education* 68 (2004): 57-62.

16. Kay Chick, "Gender Balance in Current K-12 American History Textbooks," *Social Studies Research and Practice* 1 (2006): 284-290.

17. American Historical Association, *Guidelines for the Preparation, Evaluation, and Selection of History Textbooks* (Washington, DC: American Historical Association). Available at www.historians.org.

18. Hinde, *ibid.*

19. W. Parker, *Social Studies in Elementary Education*, 12 ed. (Columbus, OH: Pearson Merrill, 2005).

20. P. Yorks and E. Folio, *Engagement Rates During Thematic and Traditional Instruction* (1993): ERIC ED 363412.

21. M. Schubert and S. Melnick, *The Arts in Curriculum Integration* (1997): Paper presented at the annual meeting of the Eastern Educational Research Association, Hilton Head, SC: ERIC ED424151.

22. A. Hargreaves and S. Moore, "Curriculum Integration and Classroom Relevance: A Study of Teachers' Practice," *Journal of Curriculum and Supervision* 15 (2000): 89-112.

23. Hinde, 105.

24. Deborah Ellermeyer and Kay Chick, "Humanizing History Through the Use of Multicultural Picture Books," *Pennsylvania Reads: Journal of the Keystone State Reading Association* 4 (2003): 18-32.

25. J. Beaty, *Building Bridges with Multicultural Picture Books* (Upper Saddle River, NJ: Prentice-Hall, 1997); P. Faris and C. Fuhler, "Developing Social Studies Concepts Through Picture Books," *The Reading Teacher* 47 (1994): 380-387.

26. National Council for the Social Studies, *ibid.*

27. National Council for the Social Studies, *A Vision of Powerful Teaching and Learning in the Social Studies: Building Social Understanding and Civic Efficacy* (Task Force on Standards for Teaching and Learning in the Social Studies, National Council for the Social Studies, 1993).

28. Esther Forbes, *Johnny Tremain* (New York: F. Watts, 1943); J. Collier, *My Brother Sam is Dead* (New York: Four Winds Press, 1974).

29. M. Barrs and S. Pidgeon, *Reading the Difference* (York, MN: Stenhouse, 1994).

30. C. Schultheis, "A Study of the Relationship Between Gender and Reading Preferences in Adolescents," Kent State University: ERIC ED 367376; Kay Chick and Rose Heilman-Houser, "Children's Literature Choices: Gender Stereotypes Prevail," *Pennsylvania Reads: Journal of the Keystone State Reading Association* 1 (2000): 3-13.

31. Mary Beth McCauley, "Matching Boys with Books," *The Christian Science Monitor*, May 24, 2005: 11.

32. McCarley, *ibid.*

33. Bronwyn T. Williams, "Boys May Be Boys, But Do They Have to Read and Write That Way?," *Journal of Adolescent & Adult Literacy* 47 (2004): 510-516.

34. Irene Smalls, *Ebony Sea* (Stamford, CT: Longmeadow Press, 1995).

CHAPTER TWO

Teaching Women's History in the Primary Grades

In many classrooms, the teaching of state history begins in fourth grade and the teaching of United States history in fifth grade. Educators and developmental theorists, such as Piaget, have long believed that preschool and primary grade children live in the moment and are able to understand no time except the present. Therefore, they concluded that young children would be unable to think and problem solve at a cognitive level necessary for historical understanding.[1]

Beginning in the 1980s, studies have contradicted the conclusion that teaching history in the primary grades was developmentally inappropriate. Egan indicates that young children have experienced such concepts as love/hate, good/bad, fear/security, and courage/cowardice, which they can then apply to an understanding of events in history.[2] More importantly, however, is the concept of time. "The most basic element in an individual's interaction with history is his understanding of time."[3]

Although young children do not fully understand historical chronology, they are able to make basic distinctions in temporal concepts such as "before," "after," and "long, long ago." They understand general chronological sequences (for example, people rode in covered wagons before automobiles) and can place historical photographs in an accurate sequence.[4] One study reported that children as young as age six are able to comprehend select historical time and history concepts, and such skill is largely dependent on their developmental level.[5]

The concept of time is an important consideration as teachers are planning history instruction for primary grade students, and time language must be carefully chosen. Children as young as age four understand past and present.[6] First and second grade children have successfully mastered time and history concepts when the activities were developmentally appropriate, interesting to students, and taught systematically and sequentially.[7] By third grade, students are consistently able to categorize pictures as "old," "older," "close to now," and "now," as well as a category

between "old" and "close to now."[8] While these studies suggest it is apparent that young children understand and use their own time language, the study of historical events and people should be introduced without dates before the age of nine.[9]

While studies have confirmed that young children are able to understand historical concepts and, in fact, have acquired a wide range of historical knowledge by the time they start school, researchers have also documented the necessity for teaching history before the fourth or fifth grade. If students have no history instruction in the primary grades, they will have no framework for the formal presentation of history when it begins in the intermediate grades.[10] To further justify the teaching of history to young children, it has been compared by some to the teaching of mathematics. No teacher would recommend waiting until students are able to comprehend complex mathematical concepts, such as algebra, before beginning the teaching of math. The same principles apply to the teaching of time and history concepts.[11]

By using age-appropriate time language and a selection of historical events that capture the interest and curiosity of young children, primary grade teachers can ensure that history instruction is developmentally appropriate. Egan suggests that it "consist of real events, real characters, real times, real places. The events should be dramatic; the characters, heroic; the times and places, strange and distant."[12] These "real" events and "real" times can be made as concrete as possible through the use of timelines. Timelines can be made manipulative, interactive, and visual through the addition of artifacts, pictures, drawings, and photographs. Narratives can then be built around the timelines so children are able to visualize and understand the human experience in history.[13]

Picture books are another resource that can be used to connect young children with important historical events. Picture books allow children the opportunity to utilize their visual literacy skills by viewing and analyzing illustrations. Students should have access to both historical fiction and biography, and books should be available in a wide range of reading levels. Picture books can be incorporated into a unit of study on a particular historical time period or event, so teachers are able to clarify objectives, build prior knowledge, and plan appropriate extension activities.[14] Picture books with strong female protagonists are an excellent tool to help young children become aware of the contributions of women in history. Children who have not yet realized the complexities and controversies of a male-dominated historical record can learn, from the beginning of their history instruction, the significant experiences and contributions of both genders.

In this chapter, primary grade students learn about women who lived from the late 1700s to the present. Themes such as slavery, women's rights, immigration, and school integration are explored through developmentally appropriate literacy activities. In addition, students find out about women who became the first of their gender to run for President, drive across the country, and serve on the United States Supreme Court. Through historical fiction and biography, young children learn the stories of women who had a positive impact on their country, both past and present. 🔊

References

1. Roy Hallam, "Piaget and the Teaching of History," *Educational Research* (1969): 3-12.

2. Kieran Egan, "Teaching History to Young Children," *Phi Delta Kappan* (1982): 439-441.

3. M. Sleeper, "A Developmental Framework for History Education in Adolescence," *School Review* 84, 91-107; citation is on page 96.

4. Keith Barton and Linda Levstik, "Back When God Was Around and Everything: Elementary Children's Understanding of Historical Time," *American Educational Research Journal* 33 (1996): 419-557; M. Booth, "Students' Historical Thinking in the National History Curriculum in England," *Theory and Research in Social Education* 21 (1993): 105-127.

5. Stephen Thornton and Ronald Vukelich, "Effects of Children's Understanding of Time Concepts on Historical Understanding," *Theory and Research in Social Education* 16 (1988): 69-82.

6. Thornton and Vukelich, 69.

7. Janet Alleman and Jere Brophy, "History is Alive; Teaching Young Children about Changes Over Time," *The Social Studies* 94 (2003): 107-113.

8. Barton and Levstik, 419.

9. Thornton and Vukelich, 69.

10. Bruce VanSledright and Jere Brophy, "Storytelling, Imagination, and Fanciful Elaboration in Children's Historical Reconstructions," *American Educational Research Journal* 29 (1992): 837-859; citation is on page 837.

11. Thornton and Vukelich, 69.

12. Egan, 439.

13. Alleman and Brophy, 107.

14. Nancy Johnson and M. Jane Ebert, "Time Travel is Possible: Historical Fiction and Biography—Passport to the Past," *The Reading Teacher* 45 (1992): 488-494.

A PORTRAIT OF COURAGE: SOJOURNER TRUTH

A Picture Book of Sojourner Truth
by David Adler. (New York: Scholastic, 1994).
Genre: Biography

Book Summary

Sojourner Truth was born Isabella Hardenbergh in 1797. Sojourner's parents were slaves; many of her brothers and sisters were sold to slave traders before she was born. She was taken away from her family when she was nine and sold to a number of different slave owners. Isabella married another slave with whom she had five children. A Quaker family paid for her freedom, and she escaped with her infant daughter. When her five-year-old son was sold to someone outside of New York, she went to court and won. She was the first African American to win a court case against a white person.

Isabella moved to New York City and worked as a servant. She changed her name to Sojourner, meaning "to move about." She traveled all over the eastern United States, speaking about slavery and women's rights. She could not read or write, but dictated the story of her life to a friend, from which The Narrative of Sojourner Truth was published. During the Civil War, Sojourner helped slaves who escaped to the north and raised money to feed African American soldiers. She was able to meet President Lincoln, President Grant, and members of Congress to propose opportunities for newly freed slaves.

Social Studies Standards
Ⓤ TIME, CONTINUITY, AND CHANGE
Ⓧ CIVIC IDEALS AND PRACTICES

Performance Expectations
Ⓤ TIME, CONTINUITY, AND CHANGE

b. Demonstrate an ability to use correctly vocabulary associated with time such as past, present, future, and long ago; read and construct simple timelines; identify examples of change; and recognize examples of cause and effect relationships.

Ⓧ CIVIC IDEALS AND PRACTICES

j. Recognize and interpret how the "common good" can be strengthened through various forms of citizen action.

Language Arts Skills
Listening, speaking, visually representing, viewing

Materials
- ▶ One copy of *A Picture Book of Sojourner Truth* by David Adler
- ▶ Black and white construction paper (one sheet of each per student)
- ▶ Scissors and glue
- ▶ Markers, crayons, and colored pencils

Procedures
Read *A Picture Book of Sojourner Truth* aloud to students. Have them respond to the following questions:

- ▶ What was life like long ago for the slaves?
- ▶ What did Sojourner do to improve her life and the lives of other slaves?
- ▶ Why did she change her name?
- ▶ What did Sojourner do to make change after she became free?
- ▶ What kinds of risks did she take?
- ▶ What words can you use to describe Sojourner? (These words can be written on the chalkboard.)
- ▶ What would she try to change if she were alive today?

Give each student two sheets of construction paper, one of black and one of another color, and ask them to make an open-minded portrait of Sojourner Truth. Ask students to draw a silhouette of Sojourner's head and shoulders on the black paper, then glue the black paper on top of the other paper and cut both pieces out into the silhouette of Sojourner Truth. On the back of the silhouette, students are to represent Sojourner Truth in words and pictures. They can describe what she believed, thought, said, felt, and did in her life.[1]

When the open-minded portraits are complete, have students share them in small groups. Encourage them to explain how their words and pictures represent Sojourner. Hang the open-minded portraits throughout the classroom.

Note
1. Modified from Gail E. Tompkins. *Literacy for the Twenty-first Century: A Balanced Approach* (Upper Saddle River, NJ: Merrill/Prentice Hall, 1997).

FLANNEL BOARD SCENES: RECREATING AMELIA BLOOMER

You Forgot Your Skirt, Amelia Bloomer!
by Shana Corey. (New York: Scholastic, 2000)
Genre: Biography

Book Summary
This picture book tells the story of Amelia Bloomer, who lived in Seneca Falls, New York during the women's rights movement of the 1800s. Working with Elizabeth Cady Stanton, Amelia helped create the Ladies' Temperance Society and was the editor of their newspaper. Amelia grew tired of wearing long skirts with hoops, petticoats, and tight corsets. She popularized a more comfortable outfit with bloomers, which was very controversial. Many people remarked that Amelia was not a proper lady. The author uses humor in both text and illustrations to attract the interest of young children.

Social Studies Standards
Ⓤ TIME, CONTINUITY, AND CHANGE
Ⓧ CIVIC IDEALS AND PRACTICES

Performance Expectations
Ⓤ TIME, CONTINUITY, AND CHANGE
   b. Demonstrate an ability to use correctly vocabulary associated with time such as past, present, future, and long ago; read and construct simple timelines; identify examples of change; and recognize examples of cause and effect relationships.

Ⓧ CIVIC IDEALS AND PRACTICES
   j. Recognize and interpret how the "common good" can be strengthened through various forms of citizen action.

Language Arts Skills
Listening, speaking, visually representing, viewing

Materials
▶ One copy of *You Forgot Your Skirt, Amelia Bloomer!* by Shana Corey
▶ Flannel board
▶ Felt in several colors
▶ Scissors and glue
▶ Two-pocket folders

Procedures
Read *You Forgot Your Skirt, Amelia Bloomer!*, including author's notes, aloud. Discuss with students the following:
▶ What kinds of things did Amelia Bloomer think were silly? (Write responses on the chalkboard.)
▶ What did she do about the things that she thought were silly?
▶ Did other people agree that these things were silly?
▶ How were the rights of women different long ago?
▶ What rights do women have now?
▶ How did Amelia Bloomer and Elizabeth Cady Stanton help to bring women more rights?
▶ What can people do to change things if they don't believe something is right?

Divide students into small groups. Give each group a two-pocket folder, scissors, glue, and colored felt. Help groups measure and cut felt to fit the entire outside cover of the two-pocket folder. Have students glue the felt in place, and then bend the folders in the middle so they stand up, creating their own flannel boards.

From the remaining felt, ask students to draw and cut out flannel board characters and props to retell the story of Amelia Bloomer. (For props, students might want to cut out a newspaper, bloomers, and signs promoting a woman's right to vote.) When the flannel boards are not in use, the pieces can be stored in the pockets.

Have students decide who will be responsible for each character's part, who will be the narrator, and who will be in charge of placing and removing the props. Give the groups opportunities to practice their flannel board retelling of the story.

Have each group perform their retelling for the class. Since a large flannel board is larger and sturdier, students can use the large size for their performances.

EMIGRATING TO AMERICA: COMPARING THEN AND NOW

Miss Bridie Chose a Shovel by Leslie Connor.
(Boston: Houghton Mifflin, 2004).
Genre: Historical fiction

Book Summary

This picture book tells the story of Miss Bridie, who chose to take a shovel with her in 1856 as she boarded a ship to come to America. She used the shovel to plant a garden, dig post holes on her farm, clean off a pond for skating, and for many other jobs throughout her lifetime.

Social Studies Standards
❶ CULTURE
❷ TIME, CONTINUITY, AND CHANGE

Performance Expectations
❶ CULTURE
   b. Give examples of how experiences may be interpreted differently by people from diverse cultural perspectives and frames of reference.

❷ TIME, CONTINUITY, AND CHANGE
   b. Demonstrate an ability to use correctly vocabulary associated with time such as past, present, future, and long ago; read and construct simple timelines; identify examples of change; and recognize examples of cause and effect relationships.

Language Arts Skills
Listening, speaking

Materials
▶ One copy of *Miss Bridie Chose a Shovel* by Leslie Connor
▶ Emigrating to America handouts (one per student)

Procedures
Read *Miss Bridie Chose a Shovel* aloud to the class. Ask students to consider:
▶ Why people in the past wanted to come to America
▶ Why people in the present want to come to America
▶ Why they believe people of the future will want to come to America
▶ Why Miss Bridie chose to bring a shovel, rather than a chiming clock or a porcelain figurine
▶ The responsibilities that women in the 1800s had when they got to America
▶ What Miss Bridie might choose to bring to America if she were coming today
▶ The difficulties and challenges that women like Miss Bridie faced when they came to America in 1856; in 2008.

Give each student an Emigrating to America handout (see page 16). Discuss the meaning of the word *emigrate*. Read the directions and have students complete the activity. Ask them to work with a partner and compare the items they chose. Students should be encouraged to explain why they chose each item. As a large group, allow volunteers to share the possessions they chose to bring. Ask students to discuss ways that each item would be useful or enjoyable in America.

Ask students to consider what it might be like to emigrate to America in 2008 and how they might arrive here. Have them brainstorm items that an eight-year-old child might bring to America if he/she was coming now. List items on the chalkboard or chart paper. Remind students that the possessions might vary depending on the country from which the child was emigrating. Have them consider how the items are like and different from those in 1856.

Name: _____ Date: _____

Emigrating to America!

You are eight years old in the year 1856. You and your family have decided to come to America. You have only a small satchel to carry onto the ship, and it will hold only 4 items. You must decide what to bring with you. Number from 1-4 the possessions that are most important or useful to you. Be ready to explain why you chose each item.

_____ A change of clothes	_____ Your favorite book
_____ Candy	_____ A candle
_____ Your favorite toy	_____ Sewing needle and thread
_____ A hat	_____ A pocket knife
_____ Soap	_____ Your pet frog

REPRESENTING TIME: HOW MANY IS ONE HUNDRED?

A Woman for President: The Story of Victoria Woodhull **by Kathleen Krull. (New York: Walker & Co., 2004).**
Genre: Biography

Book Summary
This picture book begins with Victoria Chaflin's difficult childhood. Her father beat her and her siblings, and they had little food. By the age of eight, she was helping to support her family. She married at the age of 14 to an alcoholic husband. Victoria eventually left him and traveled the country as a fortune teller with her sister. She met Cornelius Vanderbilt and gave him a stock tip that proved right. Mr. Vanderbilt shared the profits, making her a millionaire.

Victoria and her sister used the money to form the first female-owned brokerage company. She and her new husband and children invited the rest of the family to live with them in their mansion. Victoria began speaking at women's rights meetings and, in 1870, decided to run for President. She voiced her opinions in her own newspaper and became the first woman in history to address Congress about the women's right to vote. She was also invited to the White House to speak to President Ulysses S. Grant. Victoria ran for President under the Equal Rights Party, but did not win the 1872 election.

Social Studies Standards
❶ TIME, CONTINUITY, AND CHANGE
❿ CIVIC IDEALS AND PRACTICES

Performance Expectations
❶ TIME, CONTINUITY, AND CHANGE
b. Demonstrate an ability to use correctly vocabulary associated with time such as past, present, future, and long ago; read and construct simple timelines; identify examples of change; and recognize examples of cause and effect relationships.

❿ CIVIC IDEALS AND PRACTICES
a. Identify key ideals of the United States' democratic republican form of government, such as individual human dignity, liberty, justice, equality, and the rule of law, and discuss their application in specific situations.

Language Arts Skills
Listening, speaking, visually representing, writing

Materials
▶ One copy of *A Woman for President: The Story of Victoria Woodhull* by Kathleen Krull
▶ Small objects for counting
▶ Language experience paper (one piece per student)
▶ Crayons and pencils

Procedures
Read the book aloud, including the introduction. Discuss with students the following:
▶ Did women have equality long ago?
▶ Was the human dignity of women respected long ago?
▶ What rights were only given to men long ago? Why?
▶ What does our United States Constitution say about equality?
▶ Have the rights of women changed since Victoria Woodhull lived? In what ways?
▶ Have we ever had a woman President of the United States? Why or why not?
▶ Do you think we will have a woman President of the United States in the future? Why or why not?

Calculate on the chalkboard the number of years it has been since Victoria Woodhull lost her campaign for the presidency. Have students summarize what women's lives were like long ago. Ask them if they can name other things that happened over 100 years ago.

To help students understand the number 100, provide them with activities to help them experience and visually represent the number. Provide them with small objects they can count into a container until they reach 100 (crayons, paper clips, and dry beans work well). Students might also enjoy bringing in pennies from home and grouping them into sets of 100. The money could then be donated to a charity of the students' choice. To emphasize counting by tens, students could group the items by ten and then count the number of tens it takes to get to 100.

Have volunteers from class stand at the school entrance and count the people as they enter the building. The 100th person could be given a prize of 100 jelly beans or stickers.

Ask students to involve their families in a community scavenger hunt. Encourage children and family members to find artifacts and buildings in the community that are over 100 years old. Students can bring in the artifacts, or pictures of them, to be placed in an artifact center and they can discuss the purpose for each artifact. Examples of artifacts include a butter mold, a school bell, an old school book, or a photograph of ancestors. Pictures of the buildings can be taken and placed on a map of the community. Family members might be able to discover the significance of these buildings to the history of the community so these facts could be shared with students.[1]

Give each student one piece of language experience paper. (Language experience paper usually has lines for writing at the bottom and a space for illustrating at the top.) Have each student create a story about the artifacts and pictures in the artifact center. Encourage them to use invented spelling for their stories. Ask students to share their stories in small groups and post them throughout the classroom.

Note

1.   Modified from M. Gail Hickey, *Bringing History Home: Local and Family History Projects for Grades K-6* (Boston: Allyn and Bacon, 1999).

ENCOURAGING CREATIVITY THROUGH INVENTION DESIGN

Marvelous Mattie: How Margaret E. Knight Became an Inventor **by Emily Arnold McCully. (New York: Farrar Straus Giroux, 2006).**
Genre: Biography

Book Summary

This picture book highlights the life of Mattie Knight, who grew up in the 1800s in York, Maine. She lived with her widowed mother and her two brothers, and she loved to invent and build things. Mattie's family worked in the textile mills, where Mattie joined them when she turned twelve. She worked long hours, and there were many injuries in the factory. When her friend was injured from a flying loom shuttle, Mattie designed a metal guard to prevent further injuries. Her boss and her family were very impressed.

When Mattie was older, she moved away to work in several different factories. One factory made paper bags, but there were imperfections in the design. Mattie worked for two years in her basement to invent a bag with a flat bottom and the machine to make it. She traveled to Boston to the patent office, but learned that someone had stolen her design and applied for the same patent the week before. Mattie went to court and won her case. She later started the Eastern Paper Bag Company and was an inventor for the rest of her life.

Social Studies Standards
Ⓘ **TIME, CONTINUITY, AND CHANGE**
Ⓥⓘⓘⓘ **SCIENCE, TECHNOLOGY, AND SOCIETY**

Performance Expectations
Ⓘ **TIME, CONTINUITY, AND CHANGE**

b. Demonstrate an ability to use correctly vocabulary associated with time such as past, present, future, and long ago; read and construct simple timelines; identify examples of change; and recognize examples of cause and effect relationships.

Ⓥⓘⓘⓘ **SCIENCE, TECHNOLOGY, AND SOCIETY**

a. Identify and describe examples in which science and technology have changed the lives of people, such as in homemaking, childcare, work, transportation, and communication.

Language Arts Skills
Listening, speaking, visually representing, writing, viewing

Materials
▶ One copy of *Marvelous Mattie: How Margaret E. Knight Became an Inventor* by Emily Arnold McCully
▶ Butcher paper
▶ Pencils, crayons, colored markers

Procedures
Read Marvelous Mattie aloud and have students discuss the following questions:

▶ What makes Mattie different from most other children her age?
▶ How were the lives of children different long, long ago?
▶ How has life changed since Mattie lived?
▶ How important were Mattie's inventions?
▶ How have science and technology changed our lives since Mattie's time?
▶ Are Mattie's inventions still being used today?

Ask students to use their creativity to design an invention that could be useful at home, at school, or in the workplace. Encourage them to consider current needs and their ability to change people's lives with the right invention. Have them draw their design on butcher paper, label it, and write a paragraph describing how it works, what it is made of, what it is designed to do, and how it will change people's lives.

Have students share their designs in small groups, and allow peers to give feedback and make recommendations for improvement. Encourage those students who would like extra credit to actually build their invention to share with the class.

GIRL WONDER: MAKING PREDICTIONS THROUGH ARTIFACTS

***Girl Wonder: A Baseball Story in Nine Innings*
by Deborah Hopkinson. (New York: Atheneum, 2003).**
Genre: Historical fiction

Book Summary
Girl Wonder: A Baseball Story in Nine Innings is a picture book based on the life of baseball player Alta Weiss. In 1907, when Alta was only seventeen, she played for a semi-professional team called the Vermilion Independents. The story begins when Alta was two years old and threw a corncob at a cat on their farm. Her family realized what a good arm she had and soon had her playing baseball. Her father called her "Girl Wonder." She began to pitch and had soon struck out every boy in town. When she saw the Independents play, she convinced the coach that he would sell a lot of tickets because people would want to see a girl play. And play she did, in a dress! Alta played two seasons for the Independents and then attended medical school. She was the only woman in her graduating class.

Social Studies Standards
Ⅱ TIME, CONTINUITY, AND CHANGE
Ⅵ POWER, AUTHORITY, AND GOVERNANCE
Ⅹ CIVIC IDEALS AND PRACTICES

Performance Expectations
Ⅱ TIME, CONTINUITY, AND CHANGE
b. Demonstrate an ability to use correctly vocabulary associated with time such as past, present, future, and long ago; read and construct simple timelines; identify examples of change; and recognize examples of cause and effect relationships.

Ⅵ POWER, AUTHORITY, AND GOVERNANCE
a. Examine the rights and responsibilities of the individual in relation to his or her social group, such as family, peer group, and school class.

Ⅹ CIVIC IDEALS AND PRACTICES
j. Recognize and interpret how the "common good" can be strengthened through various forms of citizen action.

Language Arts Skills
Listening, speaking, viewing

Materials
▶ One copy of *Girl Wonder: A Baseball Story in Nine Innings* by Deborah Hopkinson
▶ Shoe box
▶ Artifacts such as a baseball, a corncob, a stuffed cat, a picture of a dress that might have been worn in the early 1900s
▶ Butcher paper (3 pieces)

Procedures
Wrap the book in one sheet of butcher paper so that students can't see the title or cover. Place the artifacts in the shoe box. Hang the second sheet of butcher paper on the chalkboard or a bulletin board. Make two headings on the paper: "predictions" and "truths." With the third sheet of butcher paper, make a timeline of the most significant events in women's baseball. Facts can be taken from the highlights page at the end of the book.

Show the wrapped book to students and tell them they are going to make predictions about what the book is about. Show the artifacts one at a time. Allow students to brainstorm what each artifact might mean in the story and write predictions in a column on the second sheet of butcher paper.

Read the book aloud. Show each artifact again and have students state the true meaning of each artifact to the story. Write the "truths" in a second column on the second sheet of butcher paper. Have students discuss the following questions:
▶ How close were your predictions to the true events in the story?
▶ Do you think this story is based on the life of a real person? Why or why not?
▶ Were girls and women always allowed to play sports such as baseball? Why or why not?

Read the author's note. Hang the timeline of significant events in women's baseball. Ask students to consider the following questions:

- ▶ What words can be used to describe Alta Weiss?
- ▶ Why did she play for an all male team?
- ▶ When were girls first allowed to play Little League? Why do you think it took so long?
- ▶ When was the first professional women's baseball team formed?
- ▶ How have women's sports changed since Alta Weiss played?
- ▶ What did Alta Weiss do for other women who wanted to play baseball?
- ▶ In the 2006 winter Olympics, men were allowed to ski jump but women were not. Do you agree or disagree with this rule? Why? What do you think the women ski jumpers could do to change this rule?

CREATING A TIMELINE: AUTOMOBILE TRAVEL IN THE UNITED STATES

Alice Ramsey's Grand Adventure **by Don Brown.
(Boston: Houghton Mifflin, 1997).**
Genre: Biography

Book Summary

This picture book tells the tale of Alice Ramsey and her female companions, who, in 1909, left New York City in an automobile. Alice's goal was to be the first woman to drive across America. Since her three friends knew nothing about cars, Alice was in charge of all maintenance and repairs. The roads were dirt or mud, and road signs did not exist. Alice had to either ask for directions or follow the Blue Book, a rather vague guide to roads in the eastern United States. There were many obstacles, and they became lost countless times. Fifty-nine days after leaving New York City, Alice and her crew arrived in San Francisco.

Social Studies Standards
Ⅱ TIME, CONTINUITY, AND CHANGE
Ⅷ SCIENCE, TECHNOLOGY, AND SOCIETY

Performance Expectations
Ⅱ TIME, CONTINUITY, AND CHANGE
b. Demonstrate an ability to use correctly vocabulary associated with time such as past, present, future, and long ago; read and construct simple timelines; identify examples of change; and recognize examples of cause and effect relationships.

Ⅷ SCIENCE, TECHNOLOGY, AND SOCIETY
a. Identify and describe examples in which science and technology have changed the lives of people, such as in homemaking, childcare, work, transportation, and communication.

Language Arts Skills
Listening, speaking, viewing, visually representing

Materials
▶ One copy of *Alice Ramsey's Grand Adventure* by Don Brown
▶ Butcher paper
▶ Photographs printed from the Internet
▶ Crayons and markers
▶ 8½ x 11" paper (one sheet per student)

Procedures

On butcher paper, draw a timeline from the years 1893 to the present. Label the timeline "The History of Automobile Travel in the United States." Hang the timeline on a bulletin board. Print photographs of Alice Ramsey, her automobile, and a map of her journey. Photographs are available at websites such as www. automotivehalloffame.org/honors/index.php?type=inductees and www.eyewitnesstohistory.com/auto.htm.

Read *Alice Ramsey's Grand Adventure* aloud. Ask students to discuss the following questions:
▶ How difficult do you think it was to drive across America in 1909? Why?
▶ What challenges and obstacles did Alice and her crew face?
▶ What words could you use to describe Alice Ramsey?
▶ How long ago did Alice make her journey?

Introduce students to the timeline. Ask them to guess why the timeline begins in 1893. Inform students that the "horseless carriage" made its debut at the Chicago Columbian Exposition in 1893. Have a student place a photograph of a horseless carriage beside the year 1893. Photographs are available at www. horselesscarriage.net/galleries/index.php?album=1. Ask students to determine where the following events would be placed on the timeline:
▶ 1903: Dr. H. Nelson Jackson traveled by automobile coast to coast
▶ June 9, 1909: Alice Ramsey left New York City to begin her drive (Alice's picture and a map of her journey can be added to the timeline.)
▶ August 7, 1909: Alice Ramsey arrived in San Francisco
▶ 2000: Alice Ramsey became the first woman to be inducted into the Automotive Hall of Fame

Ask students to brainstorm ways to determine how many days it took Alice Ramsey to drive across the country, since departure and arrival dates are known. Select one method and verify the correct number of days.

Give each student an 8½ x 11" sheet of paper and crayons. Have students select events in Alice's journey that they would like to illustrate. Each student can draw and color the event he/she selected. Allow students to add their drawings to the timeline.

Have students consider automobile travel in the present. Ask them questions such as:

- ▶ How did people travel long, long ago, before 1893?
- ▶ How has automobile travel changed since Alice Ramsey drove across America?
- ▶ What other ways can we now travel across America?
- ▶ Have any of you traveled across America? Was it by car, train, plane, bicycle, etc.?
- ▶ Which method of travel would be the fastest? Slowest?
- ▶ How do you think people will travel in the future?

EXPERIENCING THE LIFE OF GRANDMA MOSES: CREATING FIVE SENSES POEMS

***Grandma Moses* by Alexandra Wallner. (New York: Holiday House, 2004).**

Genre: Biography

Book Summary

This picture book tells the story of Grandma Moses, who was born Anna Mary Robertson in the year 1860. She grew up on a farm and had a wonderful time playing outside with her brothers. One winter, her pa became ill and could not work on the farm. Instead, he painted an outdoor scene on their living room wall. This experience is what got Anna Mary interested in painting, and when she wasn't doing chores, she was involved in artwork. Soon she got married and began having babies. She was very busy, but one day when she ran out of wallpaper for her living room, she finished the walls with a landscape.

When Anna Mary got older, her husband died and her children moved away. She was lonely, so she began painting. She exhibited some of her paintings in a local drugstore, where an art collector from New York saw them. In 1940, a gallery in New York displayed her pictures, which were usually landscapes of times past. Anna Mary became known as Grandma Moses, and was interviewed on both television and radio. She painted many paintings when she was very old and died at the age of 101.

Social Studies Standards
❷ TIME, CONTINUITY, AND CHANGE

Performance Expectation
d. Identify and use various sources for reconstructing the past, such as documents, letters, diaries, maps, textbooks, photos, and others.

Language Arts Skills
Listening, viewing, writing

Materials
▶ One copy of *Grandma Moses* by Alexandra Wallner
▶ Internet access
▶ Writing paper (one sheet per student)

Procedures
Ask students if anyone has heard of Grandma Moses. Give them the opportunity to look at the cover and make predictions on what the book might be about. Read Grandma Moses aloud. Have students respond to the following questions:

▶ What else was happening in United States history at about the time Anna Mary was born? (Civil War)
▶ How was life different for children who lived long ago?
▶ What words would you use to describe Grandma Moses?
▶ How did she get her name?
▶ What do you think she meant when she said, "Life is what we make it, always has been, always will be"?
▶ What emotions did she experience throughout her lifetime? (List these on the chalkboard.)
▶ How did her five senses help her to be a good painter?

Access websites such as www.gseart.com, www.csupomona.edu/~plin/women2/moses.html, and www.benningtonmuseum.com/grandma-moses-store.aspx, and allow students to view and discuss the paintings of Grandma Moses. Ask them to explain what they believe people liked about her paintings.

Have students review the list of emotions Grandma Moses felt during her lifetime. Ask each student to choose one emotion and write a five-senses poem about her using the following format:

Line 1: Associate the emotion with a color.
Line 2: Tell how the emotion sounds.
Line 3: Tell how the emotion feels.
Line 4: Tell how the emotion smells.
Line 5: Tell how the emotion tastes.

Sample Five Senses Poem:
Love is red.
It sounds like a kitten purring.
It feels like a hug.
It smells like fresh bread baking.
It tastes like homemade apple dumplings.

In small groups, have students share their five-senses poems. Encourage them to describe when Grandma Moses experienced this emotion and how they think that emotion might have affected her painting.

HONORING ROSA PARKS: THE CREATION OF COMMEMORATIVE COINS

A *Picture Book of Rosa Parks* by David Adler. (New York: Scholastic, 1993).
***The Bus Ride that Changed History: The Story of Rosa Parks* by Pamela Duncan Edwards. (Boston: Houghton Mifflin, 2005).**

Genre: Biography

Book Summaries

A Picture Book of Rosa Parks

Rosa Parks was born in Alabama in 1913, a great-granddaughter of slaves. She helped with chores on her grandparents' farm and picked cotton. Growing up, Rosa experienced segregation and discrimination because of the Jim Crow laws in the south. Through sixth grade, she attended school in a one-room school for African American children. Because there was no junior high or high school available for black children in her town, Rosa continued school in Montgomery, Alabama, and graduated in 1933. She became secretary of the NAACP. On December 1, 1955, Rosa boarded a bus and took a seat in the middle. She refused to move to the back when white people boarded, even though she was breaking the law. Rosa was arrested, and so began the bus boycott. On November 13, 1956, the United States Supreme Court ruled that segregated buses were against the law. Rosa is often called "the mother of civil rights."

The Bus Ride that Changed History: The Story of Rosa Parks

This picture book follows the events leading up to and following Rosa Park's bus ride and her role in the Civil Rights movements. Cartoon characters guide readers through the text with dialogue balloons, making this book very kid friendly. The refrain, "which was overturned because one women was brave," is included on each page that discusses life under Jim Crow laws.

Social Studies Standards
ⓘ TIME, CONTINUITY, AND CHANGE
ⓧ CIVIC IDEALS AND PRACTICES

Performance Expectations
ⓘ TIME, CONTINUITY, AND CHANGE
   b. Demonstrate an ability to use correctly vocabulary associated with time such as past, present, future, and long ago; read and construct simple timelines; identify examples of change; and recognize examples of cause and effect relationships.

ⓧ CIVIC IDEALS AND PRACTICES
   j. Recognize and interpret how the "common good" can be strengthened through various forms of citizen action.

Language Arts Skills
Listening, speaking, viewing, visually representing

Materials
- ▶ One copy of *A Picture Book of Rosa Parks* by David Adler
- ▶ One copy of *The Bus Ride that Changed History: The Story of Rosa Parks* by Pamela Duncan Edwards
- ▶ 8½ x 11" sheets of paper (one per student), with a large circle printed on the front and back of the paper
- ▶ Crayons, markers, and colored pencils
- ▶ Scissors

Procedures
Ask students the following questions:
- ▶ If you get on a bus to go across town or to another state, are you allowed to sit anywhere you want?
- ▶ If you go to the movies and there is a water fountain, are you allowed to take a drink?
- ▶ If you go to McDonald's, can you sit anywhere you want?

Tell students that long ago, African Americans were not allowed to do these things. Ask them to listen to what some African Americans experienced long ago. Read *A Picture Book of Rosa Parks* and *The Bus Ride that Changed History: The Story of Rosa Parks* aloud. Encourage students to join in the refrain in the latter selection. Have students discuss the following:
- ▶ Why were African Americans not allowed to do the same things as white Americans? (Give examples.)
- ▶ What did Rosa Parks do to change laws so African Americans could have the same rights as white Americans?

▶ Why was Rosa Parks called "The mother of civil rights?" What does that mean?

Show students some coins and discuss whose pictures are on the coins. Discuss the reasons why people get their picture on a coin. Have students examine the coins and list information that is on a coin (date, value, In God We Trust, *E Pluribus Unum*, etc.) List items on the chalkboard, and discuss the meaning of each.

Give each student an 8-1/2 x 11" sheet of paper with a circle on the front and back. Ask students to design a coin to honor Rosa Parks. For the front of the coin, have students follow the standard format for a coin, with a drawing of Rosa's portrait. On the back, have students use words or pictures to design the coin so that it honors Rosa Parks. Students might wish to brainstorm ideas before they begin their design. Ask students to cut out their coins.[1]

In small groups, have students share their coins. Encourage them to discuss the design they created for the back of the coin, explaining how it honors Rosa Parks. Coins can be hung from the ceiling, so that students are able to view both sides.

Note

1. Modified from Tracey Beard. "Commemorative Coin," in Joan Elliott and Mary Dupuis, *Young Adult Literature: Reading It, Teaching It, Loving It* (Newark, DE: International Reading Association, 2002).

EXAMINING THE LIFE OF RUBY BRIDGES THROUGH CHARACTER ANALYSIS

The Story of Ruby Bridges by Robert Coles.
(New York: Scholastic, 1995).
Genre: Biography

Book Summary
Ruby Bridges was the first African American child to attend an all-white elementary school. Her family moved to New Orleans when she was young. At that time, black and white children went to different schools by law. In 1960, a judge ordered Ruby and three other African American girls to start first grade in a white school. Ruby was sent to the William Frantz Elementary School, and the other three girls were sent to another school. Federal marshals accompanied Ruby into school, while crowds of protesters screamed at her. White parents kept their children home for many months, so it was just Ruby and her teacher in the building. One morning on her way into school, Ruby stopped in the middle of the crowd and began praying for the people who were shouting at her. She continued praying for those people, both before and after school, because she wanted God to forgive them. This picture book includes an afterword that describes Ruby's experiences throughout her schooling, as well as her current life in New Orleans.

Social Studies Standards
Ⓘ TIME, CONTINUITY, AND CHANGE
Ⓥ INDIVIDUAL DEVELOPMENT AND IDENTITY
Ⓧ CIVIC IDEALS AND PRACTICES

Performance Expectations
Ⓘ TIME, CONTINUITY, AND CHANGE
b. Demonstrate an ability to use correctly vocabulary associated with time such as past, present, future, and long ago; read and construct simple timelines; identify examples of change; and recognize examples of cause and effect relationships.

Ⓥ INDIVIDUAL DEVELOPMENT AND IDENTITY
f. Explore factors that contribute to one's personal identity such as interests, capabilities, and perceptions.

Ⓧ CIVIC IDEALS AND PRACTICES
j. Recognize and interpret how the "common good" can be strengthened through various forms of citizen action.

Language Arts Skills
Listening, visually representing, writing, speaking

Materials
▶ One copy of *The Story of Ruby Bridges* by Robert Coles
▶ 8½ x 11" sheets of paper (one per student)
▶ Crayons and colored pencils

Procedures
Discuss with students the following questions:
▶ Are white students and African American students allowed to attend school together? Has it always been that way?

Read *The Story of Ruby Bridges* aloud. Ask students the following questions:
▶ Were African American children allowed to attend school with white children in the past when Ruby was little? Why or why not?
▶ How did things change so that black and white children could go to school together?
▶ What words could you use to describe Ruby? (Write these words on the chalkboard.)
▶ What did she do to make change? How did she help black and white children to be able to attend school together?
▶ Do you think you could do what Ruby did? Why or why not?

Involve students in a character analysis of Ruby Bridges. Give each student a sheet of paper and crayons or colored pencils. Have them lay their paper horizontally, so the 11" side is at the bottom. Ask them to fold the left edge over to meet the right edge and crease the paper in the middle. Then have them unfold the paper. Now have students fold in the two 8½" sides until they meet in the middle, using the first crease as a guide.

Ask students to open up their paper so it is flat on their desk. In the middle section (which is half the size of the full sheet of paper) have students draw a picture of Ruby Bridges and color it with crayons or colored pencils. On one of the open flaps beside the picture, have students list words to describe Ruby. On the other open flap, ask them to write one important thing that Ruby said in the story. Now have students close the two flaps. On the outside of one flap, students are to describe what made Ruby brave, using either words or pictures. On the outside of the second flap, students can write why the story of Ruby Bridges is important for children who are now attending elementary school.

Have students pair up with other students and share their character analysis sheets. Encourage them to discuss what makes the story of Ruby Bridges important for children today.

DINNER AND CONVERSATION: SHARING A MEAL WITH SUPREME COURT JUSTICE SANDRA DAY O'CONNOR

Chico by Sandra Day O'Connor. (New York: Dutton Children's Books, 2005).
Genre: Autobiography

Book Summary

This picture book is the story of the first woman Supreme Court Justice, Sandra Day O'Connor. The story begins when Sandra is six-years-old and growing up on a ranch in the desert. She loves to help out on the ranch, but most of all she likes to ride her horse, Chico. Sandra is allowed to ride in the pasture close to the house, but she must watch for rattlesnakes. One day, she decides to go on into the east pasture to see a new calf. Sandra does not pay attention to where she is riding, and suddenly, Chico jumps. There is a rattlesnake ready to strike. Sandra quickly pulls the reins, and they hurriedly head for home. She thanks Chico for bringing her home safely.

Social Studies Standards
Ⓥ INDIVIDUALS, GROUPS, AND INSTITUTIONS
Ⓥ POWER, AUTHORITY, AND GOVERNANCE

Performance Expectations
Ⓥ INDIVIDUALS, GROUPS, AND INSTITUTIONS
c. Identify examples of institutions and describe the interactions of people with institutions;
f. Give examples of the role of institutions in furthering both continuity and change.

Ⓥ POWER, AUTHORITY, AND GOVERNANCE
c. Give examples of how government does or does not provide for needs and wants of people, establish order and security, and manage conflict.

Language Arts Skills
Listening, speaking, writing

Materials
▶ One copy of *Chico* by Sandra Day O'Connor
▶ Butcher paper and markers

Procedures

Read *Chico* aloud to students. Ask students if they have heard of Sandra Day O'Connor or know why she is important. Discuss the purpose of the United States Supreme Court and share the following facts with students:

▶ The Supreme Court is the highest court in the United States.
▶ There are nine Supreme Court Justices.
▶ The Supreme Court Justices are nominated by the President.
▶ The Supreme Court meets in Washington, DC, in the United States Supreme Court building.
▶ Sandra Day O'Connor was the first woman Supreme Court Justice, appointed in 1981, and she retired in 2006.

Ask students to consider the following:

▶ Why is the Supreme Court important to the people of the United States?
▶ Why do you think it took so long for a woman to be appointed to the Supreme Court?
▶ What other groups make change in our country?

Explain to students that they will be participating in an activity called Dinner and Conversation.[1] Have students pretend they are going to invite Sandra Day O'Connor to have dinner with the class. They must decide the guest list, the menu, and interesting questions they can ask during dinner.

Have students begin with the guest list. Who might Sandra Day O'Connor enjoy sharing dinner with, besides the students in the class? Have students brainstorm a list of people and write names on butcher paper. After brainstorming, ask students to narrow their list to two or three people, explaining why they believe these people would be important. Students will be using skills in compromise and consensus building.

After the guest list is established, students must decide on a menu. Have them discuss the following:

▶ What do you think Sandra Day O'Connor would like to have for dinner? Why?
▶ Since she grew up on a ranch in Texas, are there some foods she might prefer over others?

Menu items can also be written on the butcher paper.

Have students consider some interesting questions they might want to ask Sandra Day O'Connor and their other guests. For example, they could ask Sandra Day O'Connor about her life on a ranch, the incident with the rattlesnake, how she became a Supreme Court Justice, or some important decisions she made as a Supreme Court Justice. Questions can be added to the butcher paper.

For other information about the United States Supreme Court, students and teachers can check the Library of Congress website at thomas.loc.gov/teachers/supremecourt.html.

Note

1. Suzanne Mateer, "Dinner and Conversation," In Joan Elliott and Mary Dupois, *Young Adult Literature: Reading It, Teaching It, Loving It* (Newark, DE: International Reading Association, 2002).

Additional Children's Literature Titles for the Primary Grades

David Adler. *A Picture Book of Harriet Beecher Stowe.* (New York: Holiday House, 2003).
Harriet Beecher Stowe was the author of *Uncle Tom's Cabin*. Her book brought people to hate slavery, and she had an opportunity to meet President Lincoln.

David Adler. *A Picture Book of Sacagawea.* (New York: Scholastic, 2000).
This picture book tells the story of Sacagawea, a Native American woman who helped to lead the Lewis and Clark expedition. It is possible that without her help their mission would not have been successful.

David Adler. *A Picture Book of Amelia Earhart.* (New York: Holiday House, 1998).
Amelia Earhart took her first plane ride at age 23. She made several successful trips across the Atlantic before her plane disappeared on a trip around the world.

David Adler. *A Picture Book of Eleanor Roosevelt.* (New York: Scholastic, 1995).
This book highlights the life of Eleanor Roosevelt, from early childhood through her position as representative to the United Nations. A list of important dates in her life is included.

David Adler. *A Picture Book of Anne Frank.* (New York: Holiday House, 1993).
This book gives an age-appropriate introduction to Anne Frank's life amidst the forces of Nazism. Pencil sketches and watercolor drawings provide entry-level glimpses of life in a concentration camp.

David Adler. *A Picture Book of Florence Nightingale.* (New York: Holiday House, 1992).
This story highlights the life of Florence Nightingale and her work as a nurse and activist. Her dedication brought many positive changes to the nursing profession.

David Adler. *A Picture Book of Helen Keller.* (New York: Scott Foresman, 1992).
The author provides a suitable introduction to the life of Helen Keller and her teacher, Anne Sullivan. Helen's frustrations and emotions are evident, and the ways she learned new words are described.

Michael Bedard. *Emily.* (New York: Scholastic, 1992).
This picture book tells the story of Emily Dickinson, through the eyes and experiences of a fictional family living next door. Ms. Dickinson was a recluse who wrote poetry on scraps of paper through her lifetime.

Evelyn Coleman. *White Socks Only.* (Morton Grove, IL: Albert Whitman and Co., 1996).
This work of fiction is a story told by a grandmother to her granddaughter. When she was a little girl, grandma took a drink from a "white's only" fountain. She had removed her shoes and took the drink with her white socks on, thinking this would be alright.

Barbara Cooney. *Eleanor.* (New York: Puffin, 1996).
Barbara Cooney focuses on the early life of Eleanor Roosevelt. Eleanor's parents died when she was young, and she lived with relatives until she was sent away to boarding school. The headmistress became her companion, and they traveled together for many years.

M. Dahl. *Keep on Sewing, Betsy Ross! A Fun Song About the American Flag.* (Bloomington, MN: Picture Window Books, 2003).
This book for young readers relates the story of Betsy Ross, who sewed the first American flag at the request of George Washington. The book includes original song lyrics to be sung to the tune of "Yankee Doodle."

Liselotte Erdich. *Sacagawea.* (Minneapolis, MN: Carolrhoda Books, 2004).
The story of the young Shoshone woman who guided Lewis and Clark follows the historical record. Appendices include a map, a timeline, and speculations about this famous woman.

Amy Hest. *When Jessie Came Across the Sea.* (Cambridge, MA: Candlewick Press, 1997).
A teenage girl in Eastern Europe leaves her grandmother to travel by ship to America. She learns English, works very hard, and earns the money to send for her grandmother.

Deborah Hopkinson. *Sweet Clara and the Freedom Quilt.* (New York: Alfred Knopf, 1993).
This is a true story of Clara, a young slave girl who desperately wants freedom. As she sews a patchwork quilt, she includes an escape route which she leaves behind to help others.

Gloria Houston. *My Great Aunt Arizona.* (New York: Harpercollins, 1992).
Houston tells the story of her great aunt, Arizona, who was named for the state. She was born in the Blue Ridge Mountains and taught school in a one-room schoolhouse for 57 years.

George Ella Lyon. *Mama is a Miner.* (New York: Orchard, 1994).
A little girl tells the story of her mother, who is a coal miner. The text is written in prose and details the girl's thoughts and concerns for her mother's safety.

A. Morris. *Grandma Hekmatt Remembers: An Arab American Family Story.* (Brookfield, CT: Millbrook, 2002).
This story relates the bond that is shared by three little Arab-American girls and their grandmother. Grandma shares stories of Arab culture and her life growing up in Egypt.

A. Morris. *Grandma Lai Goon Remembers: A Chinese American Family Story.* (Brookfield, CT: Millbrook, 2002).
Grandma Lai Goon shares stories about Chinese culture with her Chinese American grandchildren. This book, a part of a series, includes crafts and recipes at the end.

A. Morris. *Grandma Maxine Remembers: A Native American Family Story.* (Brookfield, CT: Millbrook, 2002).
This story highlights an eight-year-old Shoshone girl and her grandmother who live on a reservation in Wyoming. The book includes history and culture, while dispelling myths about Native American life.

A. Morris. *Grandma Francisca Remembers: A Hispanic-American Family Story.* (Brookfield, CT: Millbrook, 2002).
Grandma Francisca and her granddaughter, Angelica, live next door to one another. They spend time together, during which Angelica learns about Hispanic culture. A recipe for vegetable stew and directions for a sock doll are included.

A. Morris. *Grandma Lois Remembers: An African American Family Story.* (Brookfield, CT: Millbrook, 2002).
An African-American grandmother shares family history with her grandson in Queens, New York. She shares stories of her childhood and segregation in Birmingham, Alabama.

A. Morris. *Grandma Esther Remembers: A Jewish-American Family Story.* (Brookfield, CT: Millbrook, 2002).
Grandma Esther visits her grandchildren in Brooklyn. She shares the history of Jewish families during World War II and the loss of her family.

Marissa Moss. *Mighty Jackie: The Strike-Out Queen.* (New York: Simon and Schuster, 2004).
This book relates the story of the 1931 exhibition game played between the New York Yankees and the Chattanooga Lookouts. Jackie Mitchell, a female pitcher, struck out both Babe Ruth and Lou Gehrig.

Marissa Moss. *True Heart.* (New York: Scholastic, 1999).
This story was inspired by a photograph of a turn-of-the-century all female railroad crew. Sixteen-year-old Bee gets a job loading freight and gets a chance to be an engineer.

N. Polette. *Mae Jemison.* (Chicago: Children's Press, 2003).
This beginning biography tells the story of Mae Jemison, the first African American female astronaut. During her time at NASA, Jemison conducted experiments on how to prevent motion sickness and bone loss.

Pam Munoz Ryan. *When Marian Sang*. (New York: Scholastic, 2002).

This picture book describes the life of Marian Anderson, a famous African-American singer. Although she sang for kings, queens, and Eleanor Roosevelt, she was not allowed to sing at Constitution Hall because of her race.

Pam Munoz Ryan. *Amelia and Eleanor Go for a Ride*. (New York: Scholastic, 1999).

This is a fictional account of the friendship between Amelia Earhart and Eleanor Roosevelt. They leave a party and take a plane ride dressed in their evening gowns.

Maria Tallchief. *Tallchief: America's Prima Ballerina*. (New York: Viking, 1999).

This picture book describes the life of Maria Tallchief, a Native American girl who wanted to be a dancer. She became a prima ballerina for the Ballets Russes de Monte Carlo.

E. Tarbescu. *Annushka's Voyage*. (New York: Clarion Books, 1998).

Annushka and her younger sister leave their village in Russia to travel to America. The author highlights their voyage on a gigantic steamship and their experiences at Ellis Island.

J. Thomas. *I Have Heard of a Land*. (New York: Harpercollins, 1998).

This story takes place during the late 1800s in the Oklahoma Territory, when an African American pioneer woman and her family make a new life for themselves.

Michael Tunnell. *Mailing May*. (New York: Greenwillow, 1997).

This is the true story of Charlotte May Pierstorff, who wanted to cross the Idaho mountains to visit her grandmother in 1914. A train ticket was too expensive, so May's father sent her through the U.S. mail.

Yoshiko Uchida. *The Bracelet*. (New York: Putnam and Grosset, 1993).

It is World War II, and Emi and her family are Japanese Americans who are being sent to a prison camp. Emi is given a bracelet by her best friend, but it becomes lost.

Alexandra Wallner. *Betsy Ross*. (New York: Scholastic, 1994).

This book describes the early life of Betsy Ross and the historical events of that period in history. She made the first American flag at the request of George Washington.

Alexandra Wallner. *Laura Ingalls Wilder*. (New York: Scholastic, 1997).

This beginning biography provides accurate detail about the author of the "Little House" books, including her early life in Plum Creek and her sister's loss of eyesight.

Linda Arms White. *I Could Do That! Esther Morris Gets Women the Vote*. (New York: Farrar Straus Giroux, 2005).

This picture book biography tells the story of a determined young girl who started her own business and attended abolitionist meetings. After Esther married and moved to the Wyoming territory, she encouraged legislators to give women the right to vote. The bill passed, and she later became the first woman in the country to hold public office.

Jacqueline Woodson. *Coming On Home Soon*. (New York: Scholastic, 2004).

This story takes place during World War II, and describes the experiences of Ada Ruth and her family. Her mother leaves home to find work in the city, so Ada Ruth must stay home with her grandmother.

CHAPTER THREE

Teaching Women's History in the Intermediate Grades

Formal history instruction typically begins in the fourth or fifth grade. If students in grades kindergarten through three have received no instruction, outside of perhaps Black History Month and President's Day, they will likely have no framework upon which to build new historical understandings,[1] and certainly little knowledge of women's history. However, many intermediate grade students do have some basic knowledge of historical concepts, gleaned from their home environment, independent reading, and the media. They demonstrate simple understandings of events, such as the Revolutionary War, concepts such as freedom, and documents such as the Declaration of Independence.[2] They understand the language of time (such as the words "past," "present," and "future") and can associate people, events, and pictures with those terms. Beginning at about age nine, students distinguish between different historical periods and are able to associate dates with historical figures and events.[3]

Even when students have received history instruction in the primary grades, many of them demonstrate significant confusion with regard to historical concepts and the history of women. This may be because of the overuse of textbooks, which assume prior understanding and are often compacted into male-dominated chronologies with little human interest.[4] To build such understandings, educators suggest teachers begin with historical narratives, stories that will provide students with a context of reference.[5] In addition to narratives, beginning history instruction should include an assessment of students' misconceptions, so teachers are able to confront and correct them.[6]

Intermediate grade students develop historical understandings in a variety of ways and through many different sources. Comprehension of history and time is developmental, and students in grades four through six continue to benefit from primary sources (such as maps, letters, diaries, and photographs) and artifacts (such as relics). Students need to experience the real-life aspects of historical people and events, in order to gain understanding.[7] The treatment of history as a series of names, dates, and places to be memorized will do little to spark the interest of elementary age children, and if students have already learned that this is what history is all about, then it is imperative

that they unlearn it.

The real lives of historical figures and events can be brought to life through pictures, photographs, and children's literature. One benefit of incorporating picture books into history instruction in the intermediate grades is that illustrations allow students to view and analyze images, increasing their comprehension of the story, time period, people, and events. Students can use visual cues to make estimations of the time period, or to compare the image they are viewing to other pictures or television images they have seen.[8]

Teaching children history prepares them for life in a democracy. Since democratic societies are fraught with complexity and controversy, students need to learn history, including women's history, through problem solving and the stories and experiences of historical figures. Educators suggest that students become involved in disciplined inquiry, so they can begin to learn about the past by asking their own questions. As they begin to wonder about and question history, students can begin to examine evidence and reach their own conclusions. They need to develop the ability to reason chronologically, empathize with women throughout history, determine the multiple causes of historical events, and assess the significance of events and people from the past.[9]

Above all, intermediate grade students must see the relevance of the study of history in order to maintain interest. If they feel it doesn't apply to their lives, or it's boring and unchallenging, they won't see its importance.[10] With regard to women's history, relevance is especially important to male students, who must make connections between the contributions of women from the past to their own lives. Active learning experiences, artifact and primary source investigation, use of children's literature, and real-life problem solving can inspire students to develop and maintain a curiosity about women and their contributions.

In this chapter, intermediate grade students learn women's history through themes such as the Revolutionary War, racism and the Ku Klux Klan, women's suffrage, and the Great Depression. Notable women such as Helen Keller, Eleanor Roosevelt, Frances Willard, and Bessie Coleman are highlighted; and students become actively involved in literacy activities such as story pyramids, simulated journal writing, and readers' theater performances. Through children's literature, students learn the contributions of women in history, and find connections between these women of the past and their own lives. 🔊

References

1. Bruce VanSledright and Jere Brophy, "Storytelling, Imagination, and Fanciful Elaboration in Children's Historical Reconstructions," *American Educational Research Journal* 29 (1992): 837-859.

2. Margaret McKeown and Isabel Beck, "The Assessment and Characterization of Young Learners' Knowledge of a Topic in History," *American Educational Research Journal* 27 (1990): 688-726.

3. Stephen Thornton and Ronald Vukelich, "Effects of Children's Understanding of Time Concepts on Historical Understanding," *Theory and Research in Social Education* 16 (1988): 69-82.

4. McKeown and Beck, 688.

5. VanSledright and Brophy, 837.

6. McKeown and Beck, 688.

7. Gary Fertig, "Teaching Elementary Students How to Interpret the Past," *The Social Studies* 96 (2005): 2-8.

8. Keith Barton and Linda Levstik, "Back When God Was Around and Everything: Elementary Children's Understanding of Historical Time," *American Educational Research Journal* 33 (1996): 419-557.

9. Fertig, 2.

10. Yali Zhao and John Hoge, "What Elementary Students and Teachers Say about Social Studies," *The Social Studies* 96 (2005): 216-221.

WOMEN OF THE AMERICAN REVOLUTION: SEMANTIC CHARACTER ANALYSIS

Sybil's Night Ride by Karen Winnick. (Honesdale, PA: Boyds Mills Press, 2000).
The Scarlet Stockings Spy by Trinka Hakes Noble. (Chelsea, MI: Sleeping Bear Press, 2004).

Genre
Sybil's Night Ride: Biography
The Scarlet Stockings Spy: Historical fiction

Book Summaries
Sybil's Night Ride

This is the story of Sybil Ludington, a Revolutionary War heroine. Her father, Colonel Henry Ludington, was an aide to General George Washington in the year 1777. Colonel Ludington had just heard that the British had invaded Danbury. He needed someone to call the Patriots to muster, and Sybil volunteered. At the age of sixteen, she made a 40-mile night ride through what is now Putnam County, New York. It is reported that she had the opportunity to meet General Washington, who congratulated her on her bravery. The author's note in this picture book describes the historic markers and statue in Carmel, New York, that mark the route Sybil took.

The Scarlet Stockings Spy

This picture book tells the story of Maddy Rose, who lived with her mother in Philadelphia in the fall of 1777. Her father had been killed in the Battle of Princeton, and her fifteen-year-old brother, Jonathan, had joined Washington's army. Maddy Rose was a spy for Washington's army. Every week, she surveyed the ships in the harbor to see which were merchant vessels and which were carrying firearms for the British. Then she left a secret code for Jonathan by hanging her petticoats and scarlet stockings in a certain pattern.

When the British invaded, Jonathan was involved in the Battle at Brandywine Creek. Maddy Rose learned that he had been killed, and all she had left was the blue coat he wore into battle. Maddy Rose made a flag from her petticoats, her scarlet stockings, and Jonathan's blue coat. When the British were run out of Philadelphia, Maddy Rose's flag flew in honor of her brother.

Social Studies Standards
❿ TIME, CONTINUITY, AND CHANGE
⓸ INDIVIDUAL DEVELOPMENT AND IDENTITY

Performance Expectations
❿ TIME, CONTINUITY, AND CHANGE
  e. Develop critical sensitivities such as empathy and skepticism regarding attitudes, values, and behaviors of people in different historical contexts.
⓸ INDIVIDUAL DEVELOPMENT AND IDENTITY
  d. Relate such factors as physical endowment and capabilities, learning, motivation, personality, perception, and behavior to individual development.

Language Arts Skills
Listening, speaking, viewing, visually representing

Materials
▶ One copy of *Sybil's Night Ride* by Karen Winnick
▶ One copy of *The Scarlet Stockings Spy* by Trinka Hakes Noble
▶ Semantic character analysis handouts (see page 38; one per student)

Procedures
Provide background knowledge and activate students' prior knowledge of the Revolutionary War.

Read *Sybil's Night Ride* aloud to students. Ask students to consider the following:
▶ What is a "call to muster"?
▶ How long do you think it would take to ride 40 miles on a rainy night?
▶ Did Sybil have a successful ride?
▶ How does Sybil's ride compare to Paul Revere's ride?

Read *The Scarlet Stockings Spy* aloud to students. Ask students to listen to the ways the story of Maddy Rose is similar to and different from the story of Sybil Ludington. Have students discuss the following:
▶ How old do you think Maddy Rose was?
▶ What code did Maddy Rose and her brother use? Why was it so important?

Sybil Ludington and Maddy Rose
Semantic Character Analysis

Directions: Mark a plus (+) to represent yes, a minus (-) to represent no, or a (+/-) to represent sometimes, for Sybil Ludington and Maddy Rose.

	Brave	Rode a horse	Sided with General Washington's Army	Warned others of British activity or invasion	Met George Washington	Risked their own life	Was a spy
Sybil Ludington							
Maddy Rose							

▶ Who do you think came up with the idea of the secret code? Do you think Maddy Rose's mother knew about the code?

▶ Even though Maddy Rose was not a real person, do you think there were spies like her who helped Washington's army?

▶ What role did young people play in the Revolutionary War?

Give each student a copy of the semantic character analysis handout. Have them mark a plus (+) to represent yes, a minus (-) to represent no, or a (+/-) to represent sometimes, for Sybil Ludington and Maddy Rose.[1]

In the large group, have students discuss the experiences and character traits of Sybil Ludington and Maddy Rose. Refer to either text for clarification on items with conflicting opinions. Have students answer the following questions:

▶ Do you think you could do what Sybil Ludington or Maddy Rose did? Why or why not?

▶ How do you think they developed that kind of bravery?

▶ Why do you think everyone has heard of Paul Revere, but very few have heard of Sybil Ludington?

Note

1. Modified from Deborah Ellermeyer and Kay Chick. *Multicultural American History Through Children's Literature* (Portsmouth, NH: Teacher Ideas Press, 2003).

WAS HER NAME REALLY MOLLY PITCHER? CREATING A STORY PYRAMID

They Called Her Molly Pitcher by Anne Rockwell. (New York: Alfred A. Knopf, 2002).
Genre: Biography

Book Summary

This picture book tells of Molly Hays, who followed her husband when he went off to join General George Washington's army during the Revolutionary War. They camped at Valley Forge in the winter of 1777, where Molly helped cook, wash clothes, and tend to the sick. When Molly followed the soldiers on to the colony of New Jersey, she carried the couple's possessions with her, including a pewter pitcher. On the battlefield that summer, the sun was extremely hot. During the fighting, Molly went back and forth, bringing water to the soldiers with her pitcher. They began calling out to her, "Molly—Pitcher!" That was how Molly Hays became known as Molly Pitcher.

When her husband was wounded during battle, he was unable to fire his cannon. Molly stepped in and continued firing. During the fighting, General Washington rode onto the field and noticed a woman. That night, he told Molly that she was as brave as any man, and that she had earned the rank of sergeant in the Continental Army.

Social Studies Standards
⊗ CIVIC IDEALS AND PRACTICES

Performance Expectation
j. Examine strategies designed to strengthen the "common good," which consider a range of options for citizen action.

Language Arts Skills
Listening, speaking, writing

Materials

▶ One copy of *They Called Her Molly Pitcher* by Anne Rockwell
▶ Story pyramids (one per student) (Story pyramids can be downloaded from www.curry.edschool.virginia.edu/go/readquest/strat/)

Procedures

Place the timeline of significant events in the American Revolution found at the end of *They Called Her Molly Pitcher* on the chalkboard. Point out the years 1777 and 1778, in which Molly Pitcher played a role in our nation's independence. Read the book aloud, and ask students the following questions:

▶ How was Molly Pitcher different from most other women who lived during the American Revolution?
▶ What did she contribute to our nation's struggle for independence?
▶ What words would you use to describe Molly?

Give each student a story pyramid handout. Have them use the following pattern to describe the life and experiences of Molly Pitcher:

LINE 1: Name of character
LINE 2: Two words describing the character
LINE 3: Three words describing the setting where the character's actions take place
LINE 4: Four words stating a problem faced by the character
LINE 5: Five words describing one event in which the character was involved
LINE 6: Six words describing a second event in which the character was involved
LINE 7: Seven words describing a third event in which the character was involved
LINE 8: Eight words describing the resolution to the character's problem or the outcome of his or her involvement in the events

SAMPLE STORY PYRAMID FOR MOLLY PITCHER
Molly Pitcher
Brave   Determined
On the battlefield
A woman in wartime
Brought water to fighting men
Fired her husband's cannon many times
Had the opportunity to meet General Washington
Earned rank of sergeant in the Continental Army

Have students pair up and share their story pyramids. Ask them to compare ways the pyramids are alike and different.

GIVING CHOICES THROUGH CONTRACTS: THE LIFE OF FRANCES WILLARD

Bicycle Madness by Jane Kurtz. (New York: Henry Holt & Co., 2003).
Genre: Historical fiction

Book Summary
In the 1800s, Frances Willard was president of the Woman's Christian Temperance Union and spent her life working for women's right to vote, child-labor laws, workers' rights, and kindergartens for children. In this fictionalized account of the latter portion of her life, she is living next door to Lillie, a young girl who is struggling to prepare for a big spelling bee.

Lillie's mother is dead, so she lives with her father and brother. Lillie is under pressure to adjust to the restrictions placed on females during this period in history, as well as the notion that too much physical exertion is not safe for girls. She must wear long skirts and stay close to home where she will be safe. However, right next door is Frances Willard, who is certainly not the role model Lillie's father wishes for her. Frances has just purchased Gladys, her new bicycle, and intends to learn to ride. Frances and her friend, Susan B. Anthony, believe that the bicycle will help to bring women the right to vote. Frances travels the country speaking about women's rights and the evils of women's dress, believing that dresses turn women into "trussed turkeys."

Lillie decides to go on strike, so she makes a protester's sign and leaves it for her father. They have a long talk, and Lillie's father finally agrees to allow her to visit with Miss Willard. Together, Lillie and Frances both work to meet great challenges—Lillie wins second place in the big spelling bee, and Frances learns to ride her bicycle.

Social Studies Standards
❷ TIME, CONTINUITY, AND CHANGE
❿ CIVIC IDEALS AND PRACTICES

Performance Expectations
❷ TIME, CONTINUITY, AND CHANGE
   b. Identify and use key concepts such as chronology, causality, change, conflict, and complexity to explain, analyze and show connections among patterns of historical change and continuity.

❿ CIVIC IDEALS AND PRACTICES
   j. Examine strategies designed to strengthen the "common good," which consider a range of options for citizen action.

Language Arts Skills
Listening, reading, speaking, writing, viewing, visually representing

Materials
▶ One or more copies of *Bicycle Madness* by Jane Kurtz
▶ Frances Willard student contracts (one per student)
▶ Butcher paper
▶ Markers, crayons, and colored pencils
▶ Writing paper and pencils
▶ Props suitable for monologues or skits

Procedures
Present the following speech as Frances Willard. You may dress the part or carry a protester's sign, if you wish.

"My name is Frances Willard, and I come to your fair city today to speak about the needs of our country. It is time for reform! We have young children working long hours in our factories, workers who are slaving away for just pennies, and women who are yet unable to vote! It is time for change! Let us speak of women's rights. When I was a young girl, my mother bought me a new gown. How dreadful! I said to my sister, 'My feet are entangled in the skirt of my hateful new gown. I can never jump over a fence again, so long as I live.' The belief that physical activity is not safe for girls is rubbish! It is the undergarments that women must wear that are harmful. A woman is a creature born to the beauty and freedom of Diana, but she is swathed by her skirts, splintered by her stays, bandaged by her tight waist, and pinioned by her sleeves until—alas, that I should live to say it!—a trussed turkey or a spitted goose are her most appropriate emblems. I have made change for myself and others should do the same. I bought a bicycle and learned to ride. I began to feel that myself plus the bicycle equaled myself plus the world, upon whose spinning wheel we must all learn

Continued on page 42

Name: _____   Date: _____

Frances Willard
Student Contract

Directions: Choose one of the following activities to complete your study of Frances Willard. Place an "X" in the box of the activity you have chosen, and list any students who will be working with you.

Activity #1 Compose a song to the tune of "A Bicycle Built for Two," about Frances Willard's life and accomplishments. Perform it for the class.	**Activity #2** Write a monologue or skit about the life of Frances Willard. Design props, and perform for the class.
Activity #3 Construct a timeline of events in the struggle for the woman's right to vote. Use both words and pictures. Share your work with the class.	**Activity #4** Choose one of Frances Willard's quotes from the book, explain the quote in writing, and illustrate it. Share your work with the class.
Activity #5 Write an Acrostic poem about Frances Willard or another woman who worked for women's rights. Illustrate your poem, and share it with the class.	**Activity #6** Write a story detailing what life would be like for women today, if it were not for women like Frances Willard. Share your story with the class.

I am working with the following class members: _____

_____

_____

Student Signature _____

Teacher Signature _____

Date of Completed Project: _____

to ride, or fall into oblivion and despair. I wished to have a good time. The chief wonder of my life is that I have dared to have so good a time."

Introduce *Bicycle Madness*, and explain to students that this is a fictionalized account of France Willard's life. Since the chapters are short, you may wish to read them aloud or, if copies are available, have students read them independently. Have students respond to the following questions:

▶ What restrictions and conflicts did women experience during the 1800s?

▶ Why did many people believe that physical activity was unsafe for women?

▶ What did Frances Willard do in her lifetime to enact child labor laws, make factories safe for workers, and earn women the right to vote?

▶ After Frances Willard died in 1898, how much longer did it take for women to get the right to vote?

▶ What other historical figures worked for women's right to vote?

Give students a Frances Willard student contract. Have them choose one activity to do independently, with a partner, or in a small group. They must sign and date the contract, and list the names of any other students with whom they might be working.

Give students an opportunity to display their work or perform for the class. You might wish to videotape the presentations so parents can enjoy them.

TALKIN' ABOUT BESSIE: A READERS' THEATER PERFORMANCE

Talkin' About Bessie: The Story of Aviator Elizabeth Coleman **by Nikki Grimes. (New York: Orchard Books, 2002).**

Genre: Biography

Book Summary

Bessie Coleman was the first licensed African American pilot. Born in 1892 into a segregated world in Texas, her father left the family when she was small. Bessie loved to read and spent her days studying the writing of Booker T. Washington, Ida B. Wells, and other civil rights leaders. When she was in her twenties, she moved to Chicago to find a better life. Bessie longed to be the first African American woman to fly, but no flight schools in America would accept her because of her color. She traveled to Paris to earn her license and then returned to the United States. Bessie participated in air shows until 1926, when her plane went into a tailspin, and she was thrown to her death. This picture book is written as a series of monologues by people who knew Bessie, including her parents, her siblings, her classmates, and her flight instructor.

Social Studies Standards

Ⓘ TIME, CONTINUITY, AND CHANGE

Ⓥ POWER, AUTHORITY, AND GOVERNANCE

Performance Expectations

Ⓘ TIME, CONTINUITY, AND CHANGE

b. Identify and use key concepts such as chronology, causality, change, conflict, and complexity to explain, analyze and show connections among patterns of historical change and continuity.

Ⓥ POWER, AUTHORITY, AND GOVERNANCE

h. Explain and apply concepts such as power, role, status, justice, and influence to the examination of persistent issues and social problems.

Language Arts Skills

Listening, speaking

Materials

▶ One copy of *Talkin' About Bessie: The Story of Aviator Elizabeth Coleman* by Nikki Grimes

▶ Readers' Theater scripts (one per student)

▶ Badges with names of readers' theater characters

Procedures

Introduce Bessie Coleman by sharing facts and photographs from a Bessie Coleman website found at www.bessiecoleman.com.

Explain the format of the book, and then read *Talkin' About Bessie: The Story of Aviator Elizabeth Coleman* aloud. Ask students to consider the following:

▶ What were the major events in Bessie's life, beginning with her birth in 1892?

▶ What conflicts did Bessie experience, and how did she deal with them?

▶ Did she accept her role in the segregated south of the early 1900s?

▶ What did Bessie do to make change?

▶ How did she influence our nation to move toward desegregation?

▶ What words would you use to describe Bessie?

Allow students to volunteer for readers' theater parts, and give each student a script and their name badge. The students who do not have scripts can be the audience. Have students line up in the front of the room in the order they will be reading. They might choose to face the wall and turn around only when it is their turn to read. Students can use simple props, if they wish. Have students perform the script more than once, so that all students have an opportunity to participate.

Readers' Theater Script
Talkin' About Bessie: The Story of Aviator Elizabeth Coleman

READERS' THEATER PARTS: Narrator, George Coleman, Susan Coleman, Nilhus Coleman, field hand, school teacher, Georgia Coleman, laundry customer, Oklahoma drummer, Elois Coleman, Walter Coleman, John Coleman, Robert Abbott, classmate, flight instructor, news reporter #1, Willie Coleman, news reporter #2, Robert Paul Sachs, young fan, Reverend Hezakiah Keth Hill, Bessie Coleman

NARRATOR: This story takes place in Chicago in the year 1926. Twenty people have gathered at Bessie's funeral to share their memories of her.

GEORGE COLEMAN: Bessie was born on a cold day in January, 1892, in our dirt-floor cabin in Texas. Even though some of our children had died in infancy, I knew Bessie would live. When she was small, I built a three-room house for us, something very few men of color could manage. I left my family to move to Oklahoma, but I sometimes wonder what things might have been like if I'd stayed.

SUSAN COLEMAN: I saved pennies to rent books from the library wagon so Bessie could learn to read. Every night, I would light the oil lamp and listen to her. It gave both of us great joy.

NILHUS COLEMAN: Because Mama kept house for a family across town, Bessie learned to clean, cook, and haul water. She never complained.

FIELD HAND: Bessie was very clever in the cotton fields. She hated picking cotton, but was in charge of tallying the bales of hay and making sure the family got paid for their work. Sometimes she would put her foot on the scales when then foreman wasn't lookin' so they'd make a little more money.

SCHOOL TEACHER: Bessie walked four miles to the one-room Colored schoolhouse where I taught. She was a good student and returned each year after the harvest.

GEORGIA COLEMAN: Bessie worked hard doing people's laundry so she could have an education. It was hard work, scrubbing with lye soap and a washboard, then using a red-hot iron to get the wrinkles out. She knew she wouldn't be doing laundry forever.

LAUNDRY CUSTOMER: Oh my, Bessie did good work. She walked five miles every Saturday to deliver my clean clothes, and always remembered to come to the back door, like Colored girls were supposed to.

OKLAHOMA DRUMMER: Bessie and I were students together at the Colored Agricultural and Normal University. Bessie only had enough money for one semester, but she never let it get her down.

ELOIS COLEMAN: Bessie loved to read about powerful women of color—Ida B. Wells and Madame C. J. Walker and Mary Church Terrell. She was tired of the segregated life in the south and heard about a better life up north.

WALTER COLEMAN: Bessie loved her life in Chicago, especially listening to Louis Armstrong sing the blues. She was searching for a career that was just right for her.

JOHN COLEMAN: Bessie got a job doing men's nails at a barbershop in Chicago. After five years of workin' there, I teased her that she would never fly planes like the women in France. Bessie knew immediately that she wanted a career as a pilot, and she quit her job that day.

ROBERT ABBOTT: No flight schools in the United States would accept Bessie because she was Colored. I told her to go to Paris where the French fliers would teach her. She went to a language school to learn French and sailed for France.

CLASSMATE: Bessie was the only woman and the only black person in our flight school. Because she was good at math, Bessie did very well at calculating speeds and distances.

FLIGHT INSTRUCTOR: Bessie learned quickly how dangerous flying could be. She watched from the ground as one of our planes lost an engine and crashed in flames. It never scared her away.

NEWS REPORTER #1: I interviewed Bessie when she returned from France. She spoke of her exhibition flights in Europe, and I could tell she loved flying.

WILLIE COLEMAN: Bessie loved telling kids her stories about flying. They would listen for hours.

NEWS REPORTER #2: Because of her color, Bessie had a hard time finding companies to sponsor her exhibitions. Our newspaper helped to arrange her first exhibition in America. Three thousand people attended, and boy, were they proud.

ROBERT PAUL SACHS: Our company, Coast Tires, paid Bessie to mention our name during her interviews. I was very impressed with her. She wanted to start a flying school for Negroes. Her plans had to wait, though, because she was in a plane crash and spent three months in the hospital.

YOUNG FAN: Bessie told the producers of her air show that she would only agree to do it if Colored people could come and see her. Boy, was I glad! She did spirals and flips and encouraged us girls to learn to fly.

REVEREND HEZAKIAH KETH HILL: Bessie stayed with my wife and I for two months in Orlando. We were very pleased to have her with us. I always remembered to pray for her safety.

BESSIE COLEMAN: I'll never forget my first flights in France. It was a blessing to learn to fly and to share the joy with other people of my race. You have never lived until you have flown!

RECREATING HISTORY: A NEWSCAST FROM THE PAST

Bessie Smith and the Night Riders **by Sue Stauffacher. (New York: G.P. Putnam's Sons, 2006).**
Genre: Historical fiction

Book Summary

This picture book is based on the true story of Bessie Smith and her encounter with the Ku Klux Klan in July 1927. Bessie traveled all over the south singing the blues with the Harlem Frolics. She and her revue toured in a custom train car, since most hotels would not accept black people. On a visit to Concord, North Carolina, Bessie's performance was interrupted by the Night Riders. Bessie left the tent where they were performing and faced a dozen white-robed men on horseback. She began moaning and moving her arms, and ran toward the Night Riders. The horses started to rear up, and one man's torch touched his horse. The horse bolted, and all the men took off. Because of her bravery, Bessie may have saved the hundreds of people that were in her audience that night.

Social Studies Standards
- **Ⓘ TIME, CONTINUITY, AND CHANGE**
- **Ⓧ CIVIC IDEALS AND PRACTICES**

Performance Expectations
- **Ⓘ TIME, CONTINUITY, AND CHANGE**
  b. Identify and use key concepts such as chronology, causality, change, conflict, and complexity to explain, analyze, and show connections among patterns of historical change and continuity.
- **Ⓧ CIVIC IDEALS AND PRACTICES**
  j. Examine strategies designed to strengthen the "common good," which consider a range of options for citizen action.

Language Arts Skills
Listening, speaking, writing

Materials
- ▶ One copy of *Bessie Smith and the Night Riders* by Sue Stauffacher

Procedures
Read *Bessie Smith and the Night Riders*, including the author's notes. Ask students the following:
- ▶ Why were African Americans not allowed to stay in most hotels in the south during the first half of the 1900s?
- ▶ What did African Americans experience in the south during the first half of the 1900s? You may want to discuss some of the Jim Crow laws found at afroamhistory.about. com/cs/jimcrowlaws/a/jimcrowlaws.htm.
- ▶ What do you know about the Ku Klux Klan?
- ▶ When did laws change for African Americans, and what caused them to change?
- ▶ What did Bessie do to bring about change?
- ▶ What did other African Americans do during this time to bring about change? Name some important civil rights leaders.
- ▶ What words could you use to describe Bessie?
- ▶ Have all the problems with segregation and racism been resolved, or is there more work to be done?
- ▶ What can citizens do today to rid our country of racism and segregated practices?

In small groups, have students create a newscast from the past. Ask them to imagine they are news reporters who have decided to interview Bessie Smith after her encounter with the Night Riders. Each group must construct a set of interview questions and Bessie's responses. They must then choose someone to be the newscaster who will do the interview, and someone to portray Bessie. The other members of each small group can direct the newscast and be in charge of props.[1]

After the questions are written, give groups opportunities to practice their script and interviewing strategies. Let each group perform their newscast for the class. If possible, videotape the newscasts so students can view themselves on "television" and analyze their performances.

Note
1. Modified from J. Kornfield. "Historical Fiction and Multicultural Education in a World War II Unit," in C. Bennet (ed.), *Comprehensive Multicultural Education: Theory and Practice* (3rd ed., Boston: Allyn & Bacon, 1995).

WHAT DO I REALLY KNOW ABOUT HELEN KELLER?: USING ANTICIPATION/REACTION GUIDES

Helen Keller: A Determined Life **by Elizabeth MacLeod. (Tonawanda, NY: Kids Can Press, 2004).**
Genre: Biography

Book Summary

By age two, Helen Keller had lost both her sight and hearing to a terrible illness. Helen threw temper tantrums and seemed unmanageable because she was unable to communicate. Her parents thought she could not learn, until she visited Alexander Graham Bell, the famous inventor who also taught deaf people. Bell eventually led Helen's parents to Annie Sullivan, who became Helen's teacher for many years. She learned through Braille and finger-spelling, and was found to be a very intelligent girl.

Helen longed to attend college and was able to pass the Radcliffe College entrance exams in 1899. Annie attended classes with her, so she could finger-spell all the lectures. Helen graduated with honors and began looking for ways to make a living. She traveled throughout the United States and many foreign countries, giving lectures on her life and the needs of individuals with disabilities. She also starred in vaudeville productions, did fundraising for the American Federation for the Blind, and wrote a book about her life.

After Annie died in 1936, Helen starred in *The Unconquered*, a documentary about her life. The story of Annie's dedication and Helen's determination also inspired *The Miracle Worker*, a television show that became an award-winning movie. Helen died in 1968, and her ashes were placed in the National Cathedral in Washington, DC. Organizations such as Helen Keller Worldwide continue to work to prevent blindness and assist people with disabilities. This picture book contains considerable more text than traditional picture books, making it suitable for students in grades 3 through 5.

Social Studies Standards
Ⓘⓥ INDIVIDUAL DEVELOPMENT AND IDENTITY
Ⓧ CIVIC IDEALS AND PRACTICES

Performance Expectations
Ⓘⓥ INDIVIDUAL DEVELOPMENT AND IDENTITY
> d. Relate such factors as physical endowment and capabilities, learning, motivation, personality, perception, and behavior to individual development.
> e. explain actions citizens can take to influence public policy decisions.

Ⓧ CIVIC IDEALS AND PRACTICES
> f. Recognize that a variety of formal and informal actors influence and shape public policy.

Language Arts Skills
Listening, speaking, reading

Materials
▶ Multiple copies of *Helen Keller: A Determined Life* by Elizabeth MacLeod
▶ Anticipation/Reaction guides (one per student)

Procedures
Introduce the book to students by reading the title and showing the cover. Give each student an anticipation/reaction guide. Ask them to consider what they might already know about the life of Helen Keller. Have students write "true" or "false" in the "Before" column for each statement. Ask students to make their best guesses, even if they are not sure.[1]

Read the book aloud or, if multiple copies are available, have students read some sections independently. As the book is being read and students are learning facts about Helen Keller's life, have students write "true" or "false" in the "After" column.

Correct answers for anticipation/reaction guide:			
1.	false	6.	false
2.	true	7.	true
3.	true	8.	true
4.	true	9.	false
5.	false	10.	true

Name: _____   Date: _____

Anticipation/Reaction Guide
Helen Keller: A Determined Life

Before   **After**

_____ 1. Helen Keller was born both deaf and blind.   _____

_____ 2. One person who helped Helen was Alexander Graham Bell, the man who invented the   _____
         telephone.

_____ 3. Annie Sullivan was Helen's teacher for almost fifty years.   _____

_____ 4. Helen learned through Braille and finger-spelling.   _____

_____ 5. Helen was unable to attend college because of her disabilities.   _____

_____ 6. When Helen was in her twenties, she married and had 2 children.   _____

_____ 7. Helen was a vaudeville entertainer and appeared in movies.   _____

_____ 8. Helen traveled the world raising money for the American Federation for the Blind.   _____

_____ 9. Helen met all the presidents from Grover Cleveland to Jimmy Carter.   _____

_____ 10. Even when Helen was 80 years old, she continued to help people with disabilities.   _____

[Answers on page 47]

Ask students to compare their predictions with the correct answers. Have them respond to the following questions:
- What were the most surprising events in Helen Keller's life?
- What words can we use to describe Helen?
- What people helped to change Helen's life for the better?
- How would Helen's life be different if she were born now?
- What did Helen do to improve the lives of people with disabilities?

- Can people who are not famous make positive changes for people? How?
- Can children improve the lives of others? How?
- If you had vision and hearing impairments, do you think you could accomplish all that Helen did? Why or why not?

Note
1. Modified from North Central Regional Educational Laboratory. "Anticipation/Reaction Guide," www.ncrel.org/sdrs/areas/issues/students/learning/lr1anti.htm.

LIVING THE DEPRESSION THROUGH SIMULATION JOURNALS

Rose's Journal: The Story of a Girl in the Great Depression by Marissa Moss. (New York: Harcourt, 2001).
Genre: Historical fiction

Book Summary

This book is a fictionalized journal of a girl named Rose, who lived during the depression. Growing up with her parents and her brother on a farm in Kansas, Rose's family experienced many of the cruelties of that period of history. The journal begins in 1935 with memories of the Christmas just past. The family could not afford a tree, so they improvised by placing fir branches in a bucket and decorating them with old tinsel. Rose was not expecting any presents, but her grandparents surprised her with a journal.

Rose's journal includes historical details of this period in history, such as the trial of Bruno Hauptmann, who was accused of kidnapping the Lindbergh baby, and the dust bowl of the 1930s. She wrote of the suffocation of people and animals from the dust, as well as methods used to knead bread, cook dinner, and garden, while attempting to prevent the dust from overtaking their lives. In one journal entry, Rose described the dust storm that she and her mother encountered on the way to her grandparents and the enormous amount of dust that almost overtook them.

Rose's brother, Floyd, did not like farm life, especially during the dust storms. He wanted to be a cartoon writer, and left without good-byes to seek a better life. Rose described the times they almost lost the farm and the ingenious ways their neighbors helped them to get it back. She believed that one day the farm would be left to her, and she wrote of the self-confidence she had in her ability to keep the farm going.

Social Studies Standards
ⓦ TIME, CONTINUITY, AND CHANGE
ⓦ PEOPLE, PLACES, AND ENVIRONMENTS

Performance Expectations
ⓦ TIME, CONTINUITY, AND CHANGE
b. Identify and use key concepts such as chronology, causality, change, conflict, and complexity to explain, analyze, and show connections among patterns of historical change and continuity.

ⓦ PEOPLE, PLACES, AND ENVIRONMENTS
f. Describe physical system changes such as seasons, climate and weather, and the water cycle and identify geographic patterns associated with them.

Language Arts Skills
Listening, speaking, writing

Materials
▶ Multiple copies of *Rose's Journal: The Story of a Girl in the Great Depression* by Marissa Moss
▶ Map of the United States
▶ Paper and pencils
▶ Library and Internet access

Procedures

Ask for a volunteer to find Keota, Kansas, on a map of the United States. Ask students what they know about living in that part of the country. Read the first four journal entries aloud, and have students reflect on the climate, economy, farm life, and news of the day. Have students read more about the Bruno Hauptmann trial at www.en.wikipedia.org/wiki/Lindbergh_ kidnapping and the disappearance of Amelia Earhart at www.amelia earhart.com.

Have students take turns reading the remainder of the journal entries aloud, or give students opportunities to read them independently. Ask students to consider the following:
▶ What words would you use to describe Rose?
▶ Why do you think she handled the challenges of this time differently than her brother?
▶ What conflicts and challenges did people experience during this period in history?
▶ What do you think caused the most difficulty for people during this time?
▶ What caused the dust storms of the 1930s?
▶ Has the United States experienced similar weather patterns since that time?

Provide students with a list of terms, people, and events associated with the Great Depression and this period in history. Have them choose one or more terms and find out more about them through library and Internet research. Ask students to use the information they find to write two more of Rose's journal entries. Remind students they are writing fictionalized entries that are based on true historical events. Terms associated with the Great Depression could include:

Herbert Hoover
Franklin D. Roosevelt
Eleanor Roosevelt
Frances Perkins
Stock Market Crash
Black Tuesday
Hooverville
Prohibition
Soup Kitchens
Drought
Homelessness
Health and malnutrition

After journal entries are complete, have students read their entries aloud in small groups. As the journal entries are read, have students provide their peers with historical information on the terms they chose to use. Ask peers to reflect on the creativity and historical accuracy of the entries.

ELEANOR ROOSEVELT TAKES THE LEAD: THE CONTRIBUTIONS OF FIRST LADIES

Who Was Eleanor Roosevelt? By Gare Thompson. (New York: Grosset and Dunlap, 2004).

Genre: Biography

Book Summary

This beginning chapter book tells the story of Eleanor Roosevelt, who was born in 1884 to wealthy parents. Her mother was beautiful, and Eleanor felt she was a constant disappointment, because she was so plain. She spent a great deal of time with her father, who took her to Europe twice when she was a child. Although the family was rich, Eleanor's father taught her to respect poor people and to help them when she could. She remembered that lesson long after her father died, and it became one of her greatest missions in life.

Eleanor's parents died when she was young, so she lived with her grandmother. Eleanor attended a private school in Europe, where she studied languages and spent her breaks traveling. Franklin Roosevelt, a distant cousin, proposed to Eleanor in 1903, and they were soon married. They had one daughter and five sons. Eleanor helped Franklin with races for the New York Senate, governor of New York, Vice President, and President, and took on many of his duties when he contracted polio. She visited prisons and homes for orphans and supported the Red Cross.

Eleanor became a different First Lady than others before her. She spoke across the country, wrote newspaper articles, and gave radio interviews. She knew what was wrong in the nation and spoke out against injustice. Eleanor worked for integration and withdrew her membership in the Daughters of the American Revolution when they would not allow Marian Anderson, an African American woman, to sing at Constitution Hall. She was a First Lady longer than anyone, because Franklin won four terms in office. She ended her career as a representative for the United States at the United Nations.

Social Studies Standards
⊗ CIVIC IDEALS AND PRACTICES

Performance Expectations
    j. Examine strategies designed to strengthen the "common good," which consider a range of options for citizen action.

Language Arts Skills
Listening, reading, speaking, visually representing

Materials
- ▶ Multiple copies of *Who Was Eleanor Roosevelt?* by Gare Thompson
- ▶ Library and Internet resources
- ▶ Magazines
- ▶ Poster board
- ▶ Markers, crayons, colored pencils

Procedures
Ask students to name the President who was in office longer than anyone else. Create a KWL chart on the chalkboard to introduce a discussion of Eleanor Roosevelt. Have students brainstorm facts they know about Eleanor and list them in the "K" column. Put a question mark beside any items that students are unsure about. Then ask students what things they would like to find out about Eleanor Roosevelt and list them in the "W" column. Ask students to check the accuracy of the facts in the "K" column and find the answers to the questions in the "W" column, during the reading of the book.

Read the book aloud, or if multiple copies are available, have students read independently. Ask students if any of the facts in the "K" column are inaccurate, and discuss any inaccuracies and misconceptions. Then have them answer the questions they had listed in the "W" column. Write what students have learned about Eleanor Roosevelt, that they didn't know before reading the book, in the "L" column. Have students respond to the following questions:

- ▶ How was Eleanor Roosevelt different from previous First Ladies?
- ▶ What did she do to make a difference in the lives of others?
- ▶ What words would you use to describe Eleanor?
- ▶ How did she develop these qualities?
- ▶ Why do you think she was known as the "First Lady of the World?"

Ask students to name First Ladies following Eleanor Roosevelt who have made a difference in the lives of others. If students are unable to name any First Ladies, make a list on the board of all those who have been in the White House since Eleanor's time. Have each student select a First Lady, research her contributions, and make a poster advertising her life and what she contributed to the United States and its people. Books, newspaper articles, and Internet resources can be used for research purposes. Information on First Ladies can be found at websites such as www.whitehouse.gov/history/firstladies/ and www.firstladies.org. Students can browse magazine advertisements to get ideas on designs and slogans. Discuss the slogan used for Eleanor Roosevelt, "First Lady of the World." Both words and pictures can be used to describe each First Lady, and students can use photographs from Internet websites, if they choose.

When posters are complete, break students into small groups so there are a variety of First Ladies represented in each group. Have students share their posters, telling the story of the First Ladies, their slogans, and their contributions. Ask students to compare and contrast the lives and contributions of the women represented. Post advertising posters throughout the classroom.

THE ABCs OF WOMEN'S HISTORY

All By Herself: 14 Girls Who Made a Difference by Ann Whitford Paul. (New York: Harcourt, 1999).
Genre: Poetry

Book Summary
This volume includes poems written to honor the lives of 14 heroic females. Each poem gives readers the opportunity to understand how these young women became involved in saving lives, exploration, equal rights, and daring feats. Women such as Rachel Carson, Mary Jane McLeod, Amelia Earhart, Wilma Rudolph, and Ida Lewis are highlighted. In the afterword, the author provides a brief summary of each woman's accomplishments.

Social Studies Standards
Ⅱ TIME, CONTINUITY, AND CHANGE
Ⅵ POWER, AUTHORITY, AND GOVERNANCE

Performance Expectations
Ⅱ TIME, CONTINUITY, AND CHANGE
b. Identify and use key concepts such as chronology, causality, change, conflict, and complexity to explain, analyze, and show connections among patterns of historical change and continuity.

Ⅵ POWER, AUTHORITY, AND GOVERNANCE
a. Examine persistent issues involving the rights, roles, and status of the individual in relation to the general welfare.

Language Arts Skills
Listening, reading, speaking, writing

Materials
- One copy of *All By Herself: 14 Girls Who Made a Difference* by Ann Whitford Paul
- Paper and pencils
- Library and Internet resources

Procedures
Choose a poem, read it aloud, and show the illustration. For example, you might read the poem about Rachel Carson. Ask students the following questions:
- Have you heard of Rachel Carson?
- If you have, what do you know about her?
- If you haven't, why do you think you haven't?
- What else would you like to know about her?

At home or at school, allow students time to find out more about the woman represented in the poem. Encourage them to use research sources such as books, newspaper archives, and the Internet. For example, they may discover that Rachel Carson was a marine biologist, zoologist, ecologist, and writer. Ask students to consider:
- How did Rachel Carson bring about change?
- Was she ever involved in conflict? How and why?
- What does our society do differently now as a result of the role that she played?
- Did she have power, and if so, how did she get it?

As a class, have students use the information they have discovered to compose an ABC list[1] on the woman. Students can use critical and creative thinking to select words or phrases that best describe her. The following is an example of an ABC list for Rachel Carson.

A Advocate for the world
B Biologist
C Conservation
D Determined
E Ecologist
F Food production
G Gold Medal of the New York Zoological Society
H Homestead on the National Register of Historic Sites
I Intelligent
J Johns Hopkins University
K Knowledgeable
L Loner
M Marine Biologist
N Nature
O Ocean
P Pesticides
Q Quiet
R Researcher
S Silent Spring

T Testified before Congress
U United States Fish and Wildlife Service
V Veery (a favorite bird)
W Writer
X eXperienced Breast Cancer
Y Yearned to Make a Difference
Z Zoologist

Have students read other poems from the book. Ask each student to select another woman to research, and have them use the information they discover to compose their own ABC list for that person. More than one student can write about a particular girl, or students can select a famous woman that is not represented in the book.

Allow students to pair up and share their ABC lists. Bind the ABC lists together to form a class book of famous women.

Note

1. See N. Fordham, D. Wellman, and A. Sandman, "Taming the Text: Engaging and Supporting Students in Social Studies Readings," *The Social Studies* 93 (2002): 149-158.

RABBLE ROUSERS: CONSTRUCTING A WOMEN'S HISTORY QUILT

***Rabble Rousers: 20 Women Who Made a Difference* by Cheryl Harness. (New York: Dutton Children's Books, 2003).**
Genre: Biography

Book Summary

This book shares the lives and accomplishments of 20 women in American history who wanted to make our country better. Women who worked to rid America of slavery, as well as those who fought for women's suffrage, civil rights, and opportunities in the work force, are highlighted.

Social Studies Standards

🄼 **TIME, CONTINUITY, AND CHANGE**
❌ **CIVIC IDEALS AND PRACTICES**

Performance Expectations

🄼 **TIME, CONTINUITY, AND CHANGE**
  b. Identify and use key concepts such as chronology, causality, change, conflict, and complexity to explain, analyze, and show connections among patterns of historical change and continuity.

❌ **CIVIC IDEALS AND PRACTICES**
  j. Examine strategies designed to strengthen the "common good," which consider a range of options for citizen action.

Language Arts Skills

Reading, speaking, visually representing

Materials

- One copy of *Rabble Rousers: 20 Women Who Made a Difference* by Cheryl Harness
- A wide range of biographies and historical fiction and nonfiction that details the experiences and accomplishments of women
- Gallon-size, zip-lock freezer bags, without labeling (one per student)
- Colored duct tape
- 8½ x 11" sheets of paper (one per student)
- markers and crayons

Procedures

Make a quilt from gallon-size, zip-lock freezer bags and duct tape. Generic bags work well because they typically do not have writing on them. Lay the bags out on the floor in a 5 x 5 or 5 x 6 pattern, depending on the number of students in your classroom. Use long strips of duct tape to connect the bags along all the borders. When the quilt is turned over, you should be able to open each zip-lock bag from the back to insert an 8½ x 11" sheet of paper. (The construction of the quilt can be a little tricky and may need to be completed before students become involved in the lesson.)

Read selections from *Rabble Rousers: 20 Women Who Made a Difference*. Since each selection is about two-pages long, students can read other selections during their free time. After students have had an opportunity to learn about several of the women represented, ask students to consider the following questions:

- What are some of the ways these women made a difference?
- What qualities or experiences did these women have that allowed them to make positive changes in America?
- Was there conflict involved in the changes they attempted to make? Why or why not?
- How did their contributions change history?
- Did change happen right away or did it take some time? Why?

Give each student an 8½ x 11" sheet of paper. Ask each student to choose a woman from the book or another woman in history that has made a difference. Have students design a quilt square on their paper that represents the life and contributions of the woman they chose. They can use words or pictures, and can refer to other sources such as books, historical magazines, diaries, or the Internet to find more details on the woman they selected.

When the quilt squares are finished, students can place them in the baggy quilt. Students may wish to explain their quilt square and why they chose a particular woman. The quilt can be hung in the classroom or in the hallway to represent the contributions of women in history.

Have students brainstorm women living today in their community, state, or nation, who have made a difference. List names on the chalkboard or chart paper. Ask students to consider the following questions:

- ▶ How have these women made a difference?
- ▶ What qualities or experiences have these women had that have allowed them to make positive changes?
- ▶ Has there been conflict involved in the changes they have tried to make? Why?
- ▶ Do you think their contributions will change history?
- ▶ Can young people make positive contributions in their community? How?

CREATING AN ALPHABET BOOK OF AMAZING WOMEN

A is for Abigail: An Almanac of Amazing American Women by Lynne Cheney. (New York: Simon & Schuster, 2003).

Genre: Biography

Book Summary

Lynne Cheney wrote this book to teach children how far American women have come since Abigail Adams' time. This alphabet book celebrates the achievements, rights, and capabilities of women throughout history. Each page contains quotes, illustrations, and information about notable women such as Elizabeth Blackwell, Emily Dickinson, Anna Jarvis, and Rosalyn Yalow. There are also tributes to First Ladies, trailblazers, quilt makers, and performers. Not a traditional alphabet book, the vocabulary is best suited for 3rd through 5th graders.

Social Studies Standards

- **TIME, CONTINUITY, AND CHANGE**
- **CIVIC IDEALS AND PRACTICES**

Performance Expectations

TIME, CONTINUITY, AND CHANGE

    b. Identify and use key concepts such as chronology, causality, change, conflict, and complexity to explain, analyze, and show connections among patterns of historical change and continuity.

CIVIC IDEALS AND PRACTICES

    j. Examine strategies designed to strengthen the "common good," which consider a range of options for citizen action.

Language Arts Skills

Reading, writing, visually representing

Materials

- One copy of *A is for Abigail: An Almanac of Amazing American Women* by Lynne Cheney
- A wide range of biographies, articles, and websites that detail the experiences and accomplishments of American women
- 8½ x 11" sheets of white paper
- Colored pencils, crayons, and markers
- Word processing capability
- Book binding materials

Procedures

Read *A is for Abigail: An Almanac of Amazing American Women* aloud or allow student volunteers to share in the reading. Engage students in a discussion of the following questions:

- ▶ What are some of the achievements these women were noted for?
- ▶ What words can be used to describe these women?
- ▶ How did their contributions change history?
- ▶ Are there women today who are making significant contributions to our nation's history?

Have students brainstorm a list of women in our country whose achievements or contributions have made a difference within the last 25 years. Record the list on the chalkboard or chart paper. If students are not able to think of many women, allow them time to check the library and websites for more information. They might also benefit from questioning family members on the women they believe have made significant contributions. Students can be encouraged to include women who have made a local impact.

Ask students to begin making decisions on what woman or women will stand for each letter of the alphabet. Encourage creativity as students make choices for more difficult letters such as "x" and "q."

Allow students to volunteer to write the page(s) for each letter, or use a lottery system to make these decisions. Students might also work in pairs, distributing the work load as they deem appropriate. Ask students to research the woman they have selected, using books, newspaper articles, websites, television, or interviews.

Encourage students to use *A is for Abigail: An Almanac of Amazing American Women* as a model and their own creativity to design their page(s). The text for each page can be word processed for a more professional look.

When pages are finished, bind the book to display in class. Pages might also be laminated for increased durability. Those students with artistic talent might wish to volunteer to design the cover of the book. Students can share the book with other classes and/or grade levels and discuss the ways these women are making positive contributions to our nation's history.

ADDITIONAL CHILDREN'S LITERATURE TITLES FOR THE INTERMEDIATE GRADES

Joan Blos. *A Gathering of Days: A New England Girl's Journal, 1830-32.* (New York: Scholastic, 1979).
This fictional work tells the story of Catherine Hall, a thirteen-year-old girl growing up in colonial New Hampshire. The book is written in a journal format and refers to historical issues, such as slavery.

Tonya Bolden. *Maritcha: A Nineteenth-Century American Girl.* (New York: Harry Abrams, 2005).
This biography examines the life of a free black child before, during, and after the Civil War. Family archival materials and primary documents help tell the story of Maritcha's fight for public education.

Ruby Bridges. *Through My Eyes.* (New York: Scholastic, 1999).
Ruby Bridges, one of the first African American children to attend integrated schools, tells her own story. Ruby was escorted to school each day by federal marshals, amidst crowds of angry demonstrators.

Michael Burgan. *We the People: Great Women of the American Revolution.* (Minneapolis, MN: Compass Point Books, 2005).
Written for grades 4 through 6, this book highlights women who played a pivotal role in the Revolutionary War. Their contributions to the war effort are discussed, and the author makes it clear that they had many duties, yet few rights.

S. Casey. *Women Invent! Two Centuries of Discoveries That Have Shaped Our World.* (Chicago: Chicago Review Press, 1997).
This book includes cool and practical inventions created by women during the last two centuries. Factual information is presented in a way that is both inspiring and interesting.

Penny Colman. *Mother Jones and the March of the Mill Children.* (Brookfield, CT: Millbrook Press, 1994).
Mary Harris Jones fought for the rights of miners, railroad workers, and mill and factory workers before leading a twenty day protest against child labor. In the early 1900s, children often worked sixty-hour weeks, and injuries were common. Her death came eight years before federal child labor laws were finally passed.

Karen Cushman. *The Ballad of Lucy Whipple.* (New York: HarperTrophy, 1998).
This novel tells the story of Lucy Whipple, who moved to California with her family during the gold rush. The move to California was her mother's dream, but for Lucy, a mining town was not the place she wanted to be.

R. Dungworth, & P. Wingate. *Famous Women from Nefertiti to Diana.* (New York: Scholastic, 1996).
This book begins with an introduction about remarkable women throughout history. American women are among those presented as leaders, fighters, reformers, revolutionaries, and caregivers.

Karen English. *Francie.* (New York: Farrar, Straus, and Giroux, 2002).
This work of fiction tells the story of a bright, African-American girl growing up in Alabama. Racism and back-breaking work are daily experiences for Francie, but she uses her intelligence to tutor an older boy in reading.

Jean Fritz. *The Double Life of Pocahontas.* (New York: Putnam, 2002).
This award-winning book tells the story of Pocahontas, the daughter of Chief Powhatan. Torn between two cultures, much of the information in this book comes from the journals of Captain John Smith.

Mary Rodd Furbee. *Outrageous Women of Civil War Times*. (Hoboken, NJ: John Wiley and Sons, 2003).

This book offers profiles of American women of Civil War times. Divided into four sections, the author includes reformers and writers, saviors and leaders, soldiers and spies, and first ladies.

LeeAnne Gelletly. *Harriet Beecher Stowe: Author of Uncle Tom's Cabin*. (Philadelphia: Chelsea House Publishers, 2001).

This beginning chapter book is part of the Famous Figures of the Civil War Era series. It chronicles the life of Harriet Beecher Stowe, who hated slavery so much that she chose to write about it. Stowe wrote *Uncle Tom's Cabin*, which helped many people in the north change their minds about slavery.

Kendall Haven. *Amazing American Women: 40 Fascinating 5-Minute Reads*. (Englewood, CO: Libraries Unlimited, 1995).

The author shares stories of great women who helped shape our nation. The first woman doctor, congresswoman, and social worker are included.

Johanna Hurwitz. *Anne Frank: Life in Hiding*. (New York: Avon Books, 1988).

This beginning chapter book highlights the experiences of Anne Frank during the time she spent hiding from the Germans in World War II. The book includes a timeline of important dates and personal author's notes.

Anne Kamma. *If You Lived When Women Won Their Rights*. (New York: Scholastic, 2006).

Anne Kamma shares what it was like long ago when women were not allowed to wear pants, play sports, ride a bicycle, or go to college. She then describes the changes that began in 1848 when women first fought for the right to vote.

W. Katz. *Black Women of the Old West*. (New York: Atheneum Books for Young Readers, 1995).

Katz features stories of African American women who made their way west as mail order brides, servants, army brides, and escapees from slavery. Archival photographs and primary documents add to the information on this little-known subject.

Deborah Kent. *The Vietnam Women's Memorial*. (Chicago: Children's Press, 1995).

This information picture book tells the story of the 13,000 women who served in the Vietnam War. The memorial was dedicated in Washington, DC, on November 11, 1993.

K. Krull. *Lives of Extraordinary Women: Rulers, Rebels (And What the Neighbors Thought)*. (New York: Harcourt, 2000).

This book contains brief biographies of women throughout history in chronological order. A full-page caricature of each woman is featured in each chapter.

Ann Martin. *Belle Teale*. (New York: Scholastic, 2001).

This story takes place in the civil rights era in the rural south. Belle Teale is a poor white girl whose school becomes integrated.

Carolyn Reeder. *Captain Kate*. (New York: Avon, 1998).

This novel takes place during the Civil War. Kate lives with her mama and a new stepfamily. Kate has always looked forward to the family's 184-mile canal boat trip to Washington City to sell coal. However, this year mama is pregnant, and the trip has been cancelled. Kate and her stepbrother make the trip alone, encountering risks and adventure.

Ann Rinaldi. *My Heart is on the Ground: The Diary of Nannie Little Rose, A Sioux Girl*. (New York: Scholastic, 1999).

Nannie Little Rose lives in Pennsylvania at a boarding school for Native American children. Her teacher asks her to keep a journal to help improve her English skills, and this diary tells of her struggles with a new home and culture.

M. Roehm. *Girls Who Rocked the World 2: Heroines from Harriet Tubman to Mia Hamm*. (Hillsboro, OR: Beyond Words Publishing, 2000).

This book profiles young women from America and around the world who have done great things. Also featured are 30 young women from across the United States who have responded to the question, "How do you plan to rock the world?"

Irene Smalls. *Ebony Sea.* (Stamford, CT: Longmeadow Press, 1995).
This book tells the story of the Ebo people who were brought to America as slaves from Africa. They followed their African queen off the ship, then back into the river to drown themselves. In their culture, when you die you return home to Africa, and they desperately wanted to return home.

Catherine Thimmesh. *Girls Think of Everything: Stories of Ingenious Inventions by Women.* (Boston: Houghton Mifflin, 2000).
This biography profiles women and girls who changed the world with their unique and innovative inventions. Inventors as young as ten are highlighted, with inventions such as liquid paper and space bumpers.

Linda Walvoord. *Rosetta, Rosetta, Sit By Me!* (Tarrytown, NY: Marshall Cavendish Children's Books, 2004).
This book tells the life story of Rosetta Douglass, the daughter of abolitionist Frederick Douglass. She was refused admission to an all-white girls' school, and so began her family's fight for equal educational opportunities for African American students.

A. Welden. *Girls Who Rocked the World: Heroines from Sacagawea to Sheryl Swoopes* (New York: Scholastic, 1998).
This book contains 33 short biographical sketches of young woman and their outstanding accomplishments. Scientists, athletes, political figures, and artists are featured, including many who are not well known.

CHAPTER FOUR

Teaching Women's History in the Middle School Grades

History instruction in the middle school grades often consists of a textbook-oriented approach and traditional teaching. Students read their text, listen to lectures, take notes, and prepare for tests. Often, the developmentally appropriate practices of the earlier grades are gone, and students spend their time sitting quietly completing seatwork. Textbooks are very political and viewed as the widely accepted information and knowledge that students need to have.[1] However, textbooks rarely provide multiple perspectives, and their generic nature brings little of interest to adolescents.

Many educators have called for increasing the diversity of reading materials offered to middle school history students. Diaries, letters, newspapers, and historical documents engage readers, bring numerous perspectives to historical periods, figures, and events, and provide information on notable women that is not often included in textbooks. With Internet access, students have a wealth of information to analyze and consider. They can investigate the accuracy and credibility of sources, just as historians do, as well as question the difference in viewpoint between sources. History can then be treated as a problem-solving opportunity, rather than simply a body of knowledge to be memorized. Problem-solving rarely occurs independently. Students must work together in small groups so they have opportunities to discuss, debate, and participate in consensus building. It has been said that "education is dialogue."[2] Dialogue brings about the development of historical thinking, defined as the understanding of historical people and cultures, and the decisions they made.[3]

In addition to primary source documents, historical fiction and biography can be used as a bridge between the historical content that must be taught and the interests and needs of adolescents.[4] The major challenge of adolescence is to develop personal identity and actively confront the problems of everyday life. Stories told through historical fiction and biography can help students to contemplate the human side of history, including the struggles and challenges of women from the past. Through these female characters, adolescents may gain insight into their own identity or find methods of solving their own problems.[5]

In this age of standards-driven instruction, historical fiction and biography may not be the most efficient means of teaching history, but they are certainly the most effective. Young adult literature allows students to internalize historical events and people and provides context for remembering them. It encourages students to see that ordinary people can do extraordinary things.[6]

In this chapter, students will be engaged in subjects such as the gold rush, the Civil War, World War II, and equal rights. Women in these stories were military spies, pioneers panning for gold, defenders of equal rights, and American citizens forced by their own government to live in internment camps during World War II. From young girls to elderly women, all of these characters demonstrated courage and strength in the midst of tremendous challenges.

Notes

1. Steven Wolk, "Teaching for Critical Literacy in Social Studies," *The Social Studies* (2003): 101.

2. G. Wells and G. L. Chang-Wells, *Constructing Knowledge Together: Classrooms as Centers of Inquiry and Literacy* (Portsmouth, NH: Heinemann, 1992).

3. Susan De La Paz and Charles MacArthur, "Knowing the How and Why of History: Expectations for Secondary Students With and Without Learning Disabilities," *Learning Disability Quarterly* 26 (2003): 142-154.

4. Barbara A. Illig-Aviles, "Great Moments in History: Engaging Young Adults Through Historical Fiction," In Joan Elliott and Mary Dupuis, *Young Adult Literature in the Classroom: Reading It, Teaching It, Loving It* (Newark, DE: International Reading Association, 2002).

5. D. Norton, *Through the Eyes of a Child: An Introduction to Children's Literature* (Englewood Cliffs, NJ: Merrill, 1995).

6. K. Nawrot, "Making Connections with Historical Fiction," *The Clearing House* 69 (1996): 343-345.

THE GOLD RUSH OF THE 1800S: CREATING A TOP TEN LIST

Away to the Goldfields! by Pat Derby.
(New York: Farrar, Strauss and Giroux, 2004).
Genre: Historical fiction

Book Summary

Molly lived with her Pa and her brothers on a farm in New Hampshire in the year 1848. Life was hard, there was little money, and her Pa was not good to her. One morning a neighbor rushed into the Malarkey's cabin. He poured a bag of gold dust onto the kitchen table and convinced Pa to head to California. Pa and Molly's brother, Matt, left immediately to get rich, while Molly and her lazy brother Malachi stayed home to tend the farm.

After a few months passed, Molly and Malachi received a letter and a map from Pa and Matt. They wanted Malachi to meet them in California, but Molly decided to go, too. Malachi could not be trusted to travel by himself, and Molly was ready for adventure. Molly sold what she could, locked up the cabin, and they left for Boston in their wagon. They traveled by ship, bungo, and burro to reach Panama. Throughout the journey, Molly served as a nursemaid for two little girls, in order to help earn money for the trip. A smelly, crowded cargo ship finally got them to San Francisco. Molly was glad they arrived before Malachi had a chance to gamble all their money away.

After a stay to earn more money, Molly, Malachi, and their friend, Kevin, sailed to Stockton and then hiked inland in search of Pa and gold. They panned for gold along the way and soon learned that it was very hard work for very little reward. Malachi took off on his own with many of their supplies, and, although they had not found Pa, Molly and Kevin returned to San Francisco. They both decided to start new businesses in this booming town, and their story ends with discussions of marriage.

Social Studies Standards
Ⓥ︎ⓘ︎ⓘ︎ **PRODUCTION, DISTRIBUTION, AND CONSUMPTION**
Ⓥ︎ⓘ︎ⓘ︎ⓘ︎ **SCIENCE, TECHNOLOGY, AND SOCIETY**

Performance Expectations
Ⓥ︎ⓘ︎ⓘ︎ **PRODUCTION, DISTRIBUTION, AND CONSUMPTION**
b. Describe the role that supply and demand, prices, incentives, and profits play in determining what is produced and distributed in a competitive market system.

Ⓥ︎ⓘ︎ⓘ︎ⓘ︎ **SCIENCE, TECHNOLOGY, AND SOCIETY**
a. Examine and describe the influence of culture on scientific and technological choices and advancement, such as in transportation, medicine, and warfare.

Language Arts Skills
Listening, speaking, reading, writing

Materials
▶ Multiple copies of *Away to the Goldfields!* by Pat Derby
▶ Word cards with terms important to the story (panning, San Francisco, gringos, Panama, rain forest, gambling, nugget)
▶ Internet access

Procedures
Show students the word cards, one at a time, and ask them to predict their significance in the story. Have students read the story independently, checking for the accuracy of their predictions. Ask them to respond to the following questions:
▶ How did Molly and Malachi travel to the gold fields? Were there other options? (Show students the three options used by 49ers at www.pbs.org/goldrush/journey.html.) Do you think they made the best choice? Why or why not?
▶ How would their journey through Panama be different in the present day?
▶ How are the principles of supply and demand demonstrated in this story?
▶ What was the best way to make money in towns surrounding the gold fields?
▶ Do you think Molly was typical of women living during this period in history? Why or why not?
▶ How would you describe Molly?

Divide students into groups of three. Have students write top-ten lists related to the story. Remind students that their top-ten lists should be written in reverse order of importance, with number 10 (being the least important) listed first.

One student in each group will list and describe what the group believes to be the top ten types of businesses generated near the gold fields. These students should also determine if any newly formed businesses of the gold rush era are still in existence today.

A second student in each group will list the top ten important facts the group learned about the gold rush that they didn't know before reading the book. These students should use Internet research to document the accuracy of the facts in the story.

A third student in each group will list the top ten experiences Molly had that demonstrated her strength and character. These students should also research the topic of women and the gold fields, to determine if women like Molly were a part of the gold rush.

Ask students in each group to share their top-ten lists within their group. Encourage them to share research they found on business development, accuracy of facts within the story, and women and the gold rush.

UNDERSTANDING THROUGH DESIGN: CREATING HISTORICAL FICTION COLLAGES

Girl in Blue by Ann Rinaldi. (New York: Scholastic, 2001).
Genre: Historical Fiction

Book Summary

Sarah Wheelock is a sixteen-year-old girl in the year 1861. She lives in Michigan on the family farm with her family, and spends her days on farm chores. Sarah's father is difficult and stubborn, and plans to marry her to Ezekiel Kunkle, a widower with several children. Sarah wants no part of marriage or feminine pursuits and longs to get away to a different life. She decides to run away and join the Flint Union Greys, giving her the opportunity to fight in the war between the states.

Sarah cut her hair and disguised herself as a man. In the recruitment line, she gave her name as Neddy Compton, and was soon marching to Ohio to catch a train to Washington City. Sarah was involved in battle and was also assigned to assist a surgeon, spending her days begging for food and supplies for the wounded that were being treated. She went to great lengths to conceal her identify, even changing her voice so it would sound like a man's. However, Sarah was soon discovered, and her role in the war effort changed.

Sarah began to work for the Secret Service as a spy. She entered the home of Rose Greenhow as a maid. Mrs. Greenhow was suspected of gathering military information and sending in on to the Rebels. Sarah was able to find Mrs. Greenhow's diary and discover how she was communicating with those who were betraying the Union. Sarah made one last trip home to check on her family, disguised as a man. While her brother recognized her, she was able to deceive the rest of her family. The story ends as she returns to her life as a detective.

Social Studies Standards
Ⅵ POWER, AUTHORITY, AND GOVERNANCE
Ⅹ CIVIC IDEALS AND PRACTICES

Performance Expectations
Ⅵ POWER, AUTHORITY, AND GOVERNANCE
a. Examine persistent issues involving the rights, roles, and status of the individual in relation to the general welfare.

Ⅹ CIVIC IDEALS AND PRACTICES
a. Examine the origins and continuing influence of key ideals of the democratic republican form of government, such as individual human dignity, liberty, justice, equality, and the rule of law.

Language Arts Skills
Reading, speaking, visually representing

Materials
▶ Multiple copies of *Girl in Blue* by Ann Rinaldi
▶ Magazines
▶ Poster board
▶ Glue, scissors
▶ Internet access

Procedures
Have students read *Girl in Blue*. Discuss with them the following questions:
▶ What role did Sarah play at home?
▶ What rights did she have at home?
▶ Who held the power at her home?
▶ Describe the individual human dignity afforded to Sarah at home.
▶ What roles did Sarah play after she left home?
▶ What rights did she have after leaving home?
▶ Who held the power after she left home?
▶ How did her individual human dignity change after she left home?
▶ Why were rights and power important to Sarah?
▶ In what ways was she different from other women during this period in history?

Discuss issues of equality between men and women during this period in history.

Give each student a piece of poster board. Have them find pictures in magazines and on the Internet to represent Sarah, the setting, the plot, and the conflict depicted in the story. In searching for pictures, ask students to also focus on themes such as rights, equality, power, and human dignity. Ask students to create a collage of the pictures they found.

In small groups, give students an opportunity to share

their collages. Have them focus their discussion on the themes of the story.

In a large group, have students consider the following:

▶ Have the roles and power afforded to women changed since the Civil War?

▶ How and why did the change occur?

▶ Do human dignity and power continue to be issues of concern for some women? Why?

EVALUATING CHARACTER TRAITS THROUGH LITERATURE REPORT CARDS

Behind Rebel Lines by Seymour Reit. (New York: Harcourt, 1988).

Genre: Biography

Book Summary

Emma Edmonds was born in Canada and left home when she was sixteen to get away from her father. She came to Flint, Michigan, where she decided to disguise herself as a man and join the Union army. Emma became Franklin Thompson and soon came to work in a Union army hospital in Washington. After a good friend was killed in battle, she revealed her identity to the chaplain's wife, who agreed to keep her secret.

Although working in the hospital was rewarding, Emma decided she wanted to do more for the Union. She volunteered to work as a spy and was cleared for such work by a panel of officers. During the next two years, Emma made eleven trips behind rebel lines to gather military information and secrets for Union officers. She had a number of disguises for her spy missions. Often Emma coated her body with silver nitrate and became Cuff, a slave boy. Other times she dressed as an old, Irish peasant woman, peddling goods to the southern soldiers. Emma's disguises were so clever that even those close to her did not recognize her.

Emma's spy missions came to an end when she contracted malaria. She knew she could not enter the military hospital for treatment, or she would be discovered. Instead, she traveled to Cairo, Illinois, took on her true identity, and was treated for several weeks in the hospital. Emma discovered that Franklin Thompson was now considered a deserter, so she could not return to the military. She eventually married and had three sons. Emma always felt it unfair that she was listed as a deserter, so she petitioned the War department and had her military rights restored. She even attended military reunions, where her comrades were astounded to learn she was a woman.

Social Studies Standards

Ⓘ INDIVIDUAL DEVELOPMENT AND IDENTITY
Ⓧ CIVIC IDEALS AND PRACTICES

Performance Expectations

Ⓘ INDIVIDUAL DEVELOPMENT AND IDENTITY

c. Describe the ways family, gender, ethnicity, nationality, and institutional affiliations contribute to personal identity.

g. Identify and interpret examples of stereotyping, conformity, and altruism.

Ⓧ CIVIC IDEALS AND PRACTICES

f. Identify and explain the roles of formal and informal political actors in influencing and shaping public policy and decision-making.

Language Arts Skills

Reading, listening, speaking, visually representing

Materials

- ▶ Multiple copies of *Behind Rebel Lines* by Seymour Reit
- ▶ Paper for character webs (one sheet per student)
- ▶ Literature Report Cards (one per group)

Procedures

Introduce the book to students and ask them to predict how many female women posed as men during the Civil War. Read the introductory pages aloud. Ask students to consider the following:

- ▶ Why do you think so many women wanted to be involved in the Civil War?
- ▶ Do you agree or disagree that women should not have been fighting in the war? Why?
- ▶ Consider the quote from Oliver Wendell Holmes, Jr., "Through our great good fortune, in our youth our hearts were touched with fire." What does this quote mean, and what do you think it has to do with this story?

Have students read the book independently. Have them respond to the following questions:

- ▶ Do you think this story is believable? Why or why not?
- ▶ What words would you use to describe Emma?
- ▶ How do you think her gender, her family, and her role in the Union army contributed to her personal identity?
- ▶ Why do you think she was so unselfish with her life?
- ▶ Why do you think it was important for Emma to have her military rights restored?
- ▶ Do you think you would be able to do what Emma did? Why or why not?

Literature Report Card
Behind Rebel Lines

Character Traits	Grade	Character Actions	Page Numbers from Text

Have students brainstorm character traits for Emma Edmonds. List those traits on the chalkboard. Ask each student to choose four of the character traits and construct a character web for Emma. Students will place Emma's name in the center of the page, draw lines from her name in four different directions and write one character trait at the end of each line. From each character trait, students draw three lines and write three examples from the book. For example, students would provide three examples of Emma's courage.

Divide students into small groups and have each group choose four or five of Emma's character traits to use in the literature report card. Each group must reach consensus, give a grade for each character trait based on how well they believe the character demonstrated the trait, and list the actions or behaviors that Emma demonstrated as a rationale for their grade.[1]

After the report cards are complete, have groups share their assessment and defend their grades. Encourage groups to compare and contrast the choice of character traits and the grades assigned.

Note

1. Modified from Patricia Antonacci and Catherine O'Callaghan. *A Handbook for Literacy: Instructional and Assessment Strategies K-8* (New York: Pearson, 2006).

CAN IT! INVOLVING STUDENTS IN ARTIFACT BOOK REPORTS

***Witness* by Karen Hesse. (New York: Scholastic, 2001).**
Genre: Historical fiction

Book Summary

This story is told by eleven different people and is based in Vermont in 1924. Two of those telling the story are twelve-year-old Leanora Sutter, an African American girl who lives with her father; and six-year-old Esther Hirsch, a fresh air child from New York City who spends her summers with Sara Chickering. Both girls are very much at risk when the Ku Klux Klan moves into Vermont and begins to take over their community.

People in the community have varying opinions on the Klan; some are horrified while others believe they have good intentions. The townspeople, one by one, make decisions on whether to join, and fear comes as a result of the cross burnings. Esther's father moved to Vermont to join her, and he also stayed with Sara Chickering. Now Leanora, Esther, and her father are targets of the Klan. One night, Esther was sitting on her father's lap when someone shot through the keyhole in Miss Chickering's door. Mr. Hirsch was shot, and while he recovered at a nearby hospital, the entire community wondered which Klan member did the shooting. Only Leanora was a witness for Merlin Van Tornhout, who was accused of the crime.

Social Studies Standards
Ⅱ TIME, CONTINUITY, AND CHANGE
Ⅳ INDIVIDUAL DEVELOPMENT AND IDENTITY

Performance Expectations
Ⅱ TIME, CONTINUITY, AND CHANGE
  b. Identify and use key concepts such as chronology, causality, change, conflict, and complexity to explain analyze, and show connections among patterns of historical change and continuity.

Ⅳ INDIVIDUAL DEVELOPMENT AND IDENTITY
  c. Describe the ways family, gender, ethnicity, nationality, and institutional affiliations contribute to personal identity.

Language Arts Skills
Reading, listening, speaking, visually representing

Materials
  ▶ Multiple copies of *Witness* by Karen Hesse
  ▶ Coffee cans
  ▶ Paper to cover coffee cans
  ▶ Glue or transparent tape
  ▶ Crayons, markers, and colored pencils
  ▶ Artifacts collected by students
  ▶ Library and Internet resources

Procedures

Discuss the history of the Ku Klux Klan and the three Klan movements that occurred, beginning at the time of the Civil War. Mark the three movements on a timeline and discuss each. Introduce the book and the two central characters, Leanora and Esther, and discuss Karen Hesse's writing style.

Have students read the book independently. Ask them to discuss the following questions:
  ▶ What conflicts were occurring in American history at the time of the Klan movements?
  ▶ Does there continue to be Klan activity in the United States?
  ▶ How is Klan activity different now than in the past? Why?
  ▶ How do Leanora's and Esther's gender and ethnicity contribute to their personal identity?
  ▶ How are these two central characters alike and different?
  ▶ What risks did Leanora take in coming forward as a witness for Merlin Van Tornhout?

Divide students into small groups. Each group will receive a coffee can and materials to cover the can. Ask students in each group to decorate the can to reflect a scene from the book or the theme of the book. Students will then bring in artifacts that represent events in the story and place them in the can. For example, students could use a map of Vermont, a toy train, a picture of a well, keys, and a stuffed dog to represent events in *Witness*.[1]

Have students in each group practice retellings of the story, playing the parts of key characters from the story. For example, one group member can tell her portion of the story from Esther's point of view, while another group member might tell his part of the story from Merlin Van Tornhout's point of view. The group members should use the artifacts from the can to visually represent their portions of the story. In addition to the characters in the story, each group should select one group member to serve as the narrator for the story. This person is responsible for contributing details of Klan activity during the 1920s as the story is retold. Each group can research facts on Klan activity from library resources or the Internet, to be used for the narrator's part in the retelling.

Give each group an opportunity to perform their retelling for the class. Have students compare and contrast the retellings and discuss facts shared by the narrators.

Note

1. Modified from Suzanne Mateer, "Can It," in Joan Elliott and Mary Dupuis, *Young Adult Literature in the Classroom: Reading It, Teaching It, Loving It* (Newark, DE: International Reading Association, 2002).

SNAPSHOT BIOGRAPHIES: A GLIMPSE INTO THE LIFE OF JANE ADDAMS

Jane Addams: *Champion of Democracy* by Judith Bloom Fradin and Dennis Brindell Fradin. (New York: Clarion Books, 2006).
Genre: Biography

Book Summary

Jane Addams graduated from Rockford Female Seminary in 1881 and wondered what she should do with the rest of her life. When her father died and left money to her in his will, she entered medical school, but soon withdrew from school because of physical and emotional problems. She made two trips to Europe and toured a settlement house in London. Upon her return, Jane opened Hull House in a poor section of Chicago. Hull House provided shelter for many of Chicago's poorest residents and gave them opportunities to explore artistic and theatrical talents.

In Jane's later years, she was a suffragist and civil rights activist. She helped to found the National Association for the Advancement of Colored People and the American Civil Liberties Union. Jane also became known as a pacifist and earned international recognition for her pacifist activities. She won the Nobel Peace Prize in 1931. Many photographs and original documents help students to learn much about this period in history and the life of this remarkable woman.

Social Studies Standards

Ⓥ**I** **POWER, AUTHORITY, AND GOVERNANCE**
Ⓧ **CIVIC IDEALS AND PRACTICES**

Performance Expectations

Ⓥ**I** **POWER, AUTHORITY, AND GOVERNANCE**
   h. Explain and apply concepts such as power, role, status, justice, and influence to the examination of persistent issues and social problems.

Ⓧ **CIVIC IDEALS AND PRACTICES**
   e. Explain and analyze various forms of citizen action that influence public policy decisions.
   f. Identify and explain the roles of formal and informal political actors in influencing and shaping public policy and decision-making.

Language Arts Skills

Reading, speaking, visually representing, writing, viewing

Materials

- ▶ Multiple copies of *Jane Addams: Champion of Democracy* by Judith Bloom Fradin and Dennis Brindell Fradin
- ▶ Library and website resources
- ▶ 8½ x 11" sheets of white paper
- ▶ Colored pencils, crayons, markers
- ▶ Word processing capability

Procedures

Give students opportunities to read *Jane Addams: Champion of Democracy* or read portions aloud in class. Engage students in a discussion of topics such as:

- ▶ The social problems Jane was most interested in
- ▶ The power and influence she had and the ways they helped her to bring about change
- ▶ Ways she influenced public and government policy
- ▶ Reasons why the book describes her as a champion of democracy

Have students create a snapshot biography of Jane's life.[1] In a snapshot biography, students consider an individual's life and select the events they deem important enough to draw and write about. First, ask students to research Jane's life and accomplishments in more detail, using library and Internet resources. Students then brainstorm a list of the more significant events in her life. Brainstorming can be done in large or small groups and documented on the chalkboard.

Have students individually select what they believe to be the most significant events in Jane's life. Ask them to create snapshots of these events that are composed of illustrations, captions, and sidebars with additional information. Sidebars are columns of information that provide readers with more knowledge on a topic, define words important to the biography, or provide quotations. They are included alongside the illustration. The snapshots are arranged in chronological order, and the student authors write a summary statement that provides readers with the theme of that person's life. Captions, sidebars, and summary statements can be word processed for a more professional look.

Give students opportunities to share their snapshot biographies of Jane Addams with peers or other classes. They can also be laminated and bound together into a class book.

Note

1. See Myra Zarnowski, *History Makers: A Questioning Approach to Reading and Writing Biographies* (Portsmouth, NH: Heinemann, 2003).

SENTENCE STEM SCRAMBLE: THE FIGHT FOR INTEGRATION

Fight On! Mary Church Terrell's Battle for Integration **by Dennis Brindell Fradin and Judith Bloom Fradin. (New York: Clarion, 2003).**
Genre: Biography

Book Summary

Mary Eliza Church was born in Tennessee in 1863, during the Civil War. Her parents had spent most of their lives as slaves. However, her father owned and operated a saloon and other properties and soon became wealthy. Mary's parents shielded her from racist attitudes and segregated practices as much as possible. She attended a private school in Ohio and was accepted at Oberlin College. Mary preferred the "gentleman's courses," such as Latin, French, and English literature, rather than the simpler courses that ladies took.

On a visit to Washington, DC, Mary met Frederick Douglass, the famous civil rights leader. They became friends, and Douglass came to have a significant impact on Mary's life. She taught at the M Street Colored High School and later spent two years studying in Europe. She married Robert Terrell in 1891 and helped found the National Association for the Advancement of Colored People. As a famous black woman, Mary felt that she represented her entire race, so she began traveling the country to speak on issues of civil rights.

Mary became involved in the woman's right to vote and was friends with Susan B. Anthony. She wrote many articles about civil rights and women's rights and was an American delegate to peace conferences during World War I. Her autobiography, *A Colored Woman in a White World*, was published in 1940. When she was 86, Mary invited friends to eat with her in Thompson's Cafeteria in Washington, DC, during the Jim Crow era. The cafeteria refused to serve them, and the case went to the Supreme Court, after which all restaurants in Washington were ordered to serve black customers. Mary remained active in civil rights issues well into her nineties.

Social Studies Standards
Ⅱ TIME, CONTINUITY, AND CHANGE
Ⅳ INDIVIDUAL DEVELOPMENT AND IDENTITY
Ⅹ CIVIC IDEALS AND PRACTICES

Performance Expectations
Ⅱ TIME, CONTINUITY, AND CHANGE
   b. Identify and use key concepts such as chronology, causality, change, conflict, and complexity to explain, analyze, and show connections among patterns of historical change and continuity.
Ⅳ INDIVIDUAL DEVELOPMENT AND IDENTITY
   d. Relate such factors as physical endowment and capabilities, learning, motivation, personality, perception, and behavior to individual development.
Ⅹ CIVIC IDEALS AND PRACTICES
   e. Explain and analyze various forms of citizen action that influence public policy decisions.

Language Arts Skills
Reading, speaking, writing, listening

Materials
▶ Multiple copies of *Fight On! Mary Church Terrell's Battle for Integration* by Dennis Brindell Fradin and Judith Bloom Fradin
▶ Butcher paper

Procedures
Read the introduction, "Who Was Mary Church Terrell?" and Chapter One aloud. Have students read the remaining chapters independently.

Write sentence stems related to the book on separate sheets of butcher paper, and post them around the room. Sentence stems from *Fight On! Mary Church Terrell's Battle for Integration* might include

▶ Mary can be described as…
▶ Mary became a crusader for equal rights because…
▶ Mary made change by…
▶ If I were Mary Church Terrell…
▶ Gender was an issue in Mary's life because…
▶ The first half of the twentieth century was a complex time in our nation's history because…

Cover the sentence stems so students are not able to read them.

Divide students into the same number of groups as there are sentence stems. Each group begins at a different sentence stem. When you say "go," students uncover the sentence stem and have one minute to write responses on the butcher paper. All group members must write at the same time, and no one is allowed to stop and read what others have written. When one minute is up, all groups rotate clockwise to the next sentence stem. Groups continue to rotate until all students have responded to all the sentence stems. Then, one-minute rotations begin again, so students have an opportunity to read everyone's responses.

To process the activity, have each group stay at their last sentence stem. Ask students to discuss the responses and write one or two summary sentences on another sheet of butcher paper. Ask students to write in large print so their sentences can be read from across the room. Each group must select a spokesperson, and then the rest of the group members may sit down. The spokesperson from each group discusses their summary and any interesting reactions to the sentence stem. Facilitate discussion of common themes and points of disagreement.[1]

Ask students to consider ways they can make a difference in the 21st century. Have them analyze their own personal qualities to discover whether their character is similar to Mary Church Terrell's.

Note

1. Modified from Rose-Colley, Bechtel, and Cinelli, "Using Graffiti to Uncover Values," *Health Educator* 26 (1994): 269.

BOOK DETECTIVES: EXPLORING THE LIFE OF MARIAN ANDERSON

***The Voice that Challenged a Nation: Marian Anderson and the Struggle for Equal Rights* by Russell Freedman. (New York: Clarion, 2004).**
Genre: Biography

Book Summary

Marian Anderson was born in 1897 and grew up in Philadelphia. She had the advantage of living in an integrated neighborhood and attending a racially mixed elementary school, although all of her teachers were white. She developed her love of singing at church and taught herself to play piano because there was no money for lessons. Marian had her first real experience with discrimination when she attempted to enroll at a high school for musically talented students. She was told, "We don't take colored." (p. 12)

Marian finally did attend high school, and her church and the black community helped with the funding. She graduated at age 24. By this time, Marian was performing in recitals and singing professionally. She and her mother traveled by train (in the Jim Crow coach) all along the east coast and throughout the south. Marian won a singing contest in 1924, and that opened the door for international engagements and study.

However, even after Eleanor Roosevelt invited her to sing at the White House in 1936, Marian was still not allowed to perform at Constitution Hall because of her race. Instead, she decided to give a free concert at the Lincoln Memorial on Easter Sunday, 1939. In attendance were members of her family, members of Congress, Supreme Court justices, and people as far as she could see. That concert was considered a milestone in the struggle for equal rights, and the membership of the NAACP doubled within a year. Marian became the first soloist at the Metropolitan Opera in New York City. She received the Presidential Medal of Freedom, the Congressional Gold Medal, and the Eleanor Roosevelt Human Rights Award.

Social Studies Standards
❶ TIME, CONTINUITY, AND CHANGE
❿ CIVIC IDEALS AND PRACTICES

Performance Expectations
❶ TIME, CONTINUITY, AND CHANGE
    b. Identify and use key concepts such as chronology,

causality, change, conflict, and complexity to explain, analyze, and show connections among patterns of historical change and continuity.

❿ CIVIC IDEALS AND PRACTICES
    j. Examine strategies designed to strengthen the "common good," which consider a range of options for citizen action.

Language Arts Skills
Listening, speaking, reading

Materials
▶ Multiple copies of *The Voice that Challenged a Nation: Marian Anderson and the Struggle for Equal Rights* by Russell Freedman
▶ Book Detective Handouts (one per student)

Procedures
Prior to students reading the book, give each student a copy of the Book Detective Handout. Have them find someone who fits each of the descriptors and get their signature. Signatures can come from people at school, home, or the community. You may also decide to allow students to use names of people who are not easily accessible, such as relatives in another state or people who have passed away. In addition to getting signatures, students should take the opportunity to talk with each person and take notes on their experiences. For example, if they know someone who has studied in a foreign country, they might want to inquire about the country, the school, the person's major, and the person's thoughts and experiences. Students may not be able to find people for all 20 descriptors, but should be encouraged to find as many as they are able.[1]

When students bring in their signatures and notes, encourage discussion and critical thinking. Have them consider questions such as:

▶ What did you learn about people who travel for a living?
▶ What did you learn about people who have traveled or studied in a foreign country?
▶ What did you learn about people who are performers?
▶ What did you learn about people who have experienced prejudice and discrimination?

Book Detectives

Find someone who:

Has been to the Lincoln Memorial

Has won an award

Has two sisters

Has experienced prejudice and discrimination

Taught themselves to play an instrument

Had a father who died at an early age

Was very committed to finishing high school

Traveled often to make a living

Has won a contest

Has lived in a foreign country

Has sailed on a ship

Has studied in a foreign country

Has met a government official

Has performed in front of an audience

Has taken a stand for something they believe in

Has traveled by train

Didn't get married until they were in their 40s

Has been to an opera

Has made a difference in the lives of others

Loves to sing

▶ What did you learn about people who have made a difference in the lives of others?

Based on these questions, have students make predictions about what they think the book they are going to read will be about. They might make predictions about the characters, the setting, the plot, and the time in which the story took place. Predictions can be recorded on the chalkboard or on newsprint paper.

Introduce the book to students by reading the title and showing the cover. Assess students' prior knowledge of Marian Anderson. Read the two pages of Chapter One aloud (the Easter Concert of April 9, 1939), and ask students why they think this event was significant in our nation's history.

Allow opportunities for students to read the book independently. In small groups, have them discuss the following questions:

▶ How were Marian's experiences similar to and different from the people you interviewed?

▶ What kinds of conflicts did Marian experience?
▶ How did Marian effect change?
▶ How does the chronology of events in Marian's life correspond to other figures in the civil rights movement?
▶ How are the rights of individuals different today because of people like Marian?
▶ What types of prejudice and discrimination still exist?
▶ What actions can citizens take to further the cause of equal rights?

Encourage students to share their responses with the large group. Engage them in a discussion of other groups that continue to struggle with equal rights issues, such as women and the aged.

Note

1. Adapted from Audrey Quinlan, "Book Detectives," in *Young Adult Literature in the Classroom: Reading It, Teaching It, Loving It*, eds. Joan Elliott and Mary Dupuis (Newark, DE: International Reading Association, 2002).

WOMEN ON THE HOME FRONT IN WORLD WAR II: ORGANIZING INFORMATION THROUGH DATA CHARTS

***Rosie the Riveter: Women Working on the Home Front in World War II* by Penny Colman. (New York: Crown, 1995).**
Genre: Information, Nonfiction

Book Summary

This nonfiction book gives a detailed account of the role women played in the workforce during World War II. The author begins with a summary of the war, invasions in Europe, and the response from the United States. Subsequent chapters describe ways life changed in America, opportunities for women during the war, and female pioneers in the workplace. Photographs, lists of women's wartime jobs, facts and figures on women war workers, and a chronology of the war make this book a valuable resource.

Shortages and rationing became a part of life in the United States during World War II, and Americans were encouraged to buy war bonds. People listened to war news on the radio, and there were war movies to see at theatres. Patriotism was the theme of the day. Extraordinary job opportunities were suddenly available for women, and many women who formerly were housewives were now in the workforce. More than six million women took jobs outside the home as welders, mechanics, and electricians. Another three million women served as Red Cross volunteers. "Rosie the Riveter," the title of a song released in 1943, became the banner for women who took wartime jobs. Although many of these women were laid off when the war ended, stereotypical barriers were lowered, and women had the opportunity to prove what they could do for their country.

Social Studies Standards
Ⅱ TIME, CONTINUITY, AND CHANGE
Ⅶ PRODUCTION, DISTRIBUTION, AND CONSUMPTION

Performance Expectations
Ⅱ TIME, CONTINUITY, AND CHANGE
c. Identify and describe selected historical periods and patterns of change within and across cultures, ...
Ⅶ PRODUCTION, DISTRIBUTION, AND CONSUMPTION
a. Give and explain examples of ways that economic systems structure choices about how goods and services are to be produced and distributed.

Language Arts Skills
Reading, speaking, writing, visually representing

Materials
▶ Multiple copies of *Rosie the Riveter: Women Working on the Home Front in World War II* by Penny Colman
▶ Women and World War II data charts (one per student)
▶ Butcher paper and markers

Procedures
Recite or sing the words to "Rosie the Riveter," found on pages 15-16 in the book. Ask students if they know when the song was written or who the song is about. Show them the cover of the book. Have students tell what they know about Rosie the Riveter and her significance during World War II.

Give each student a Women and World War II data chart. Tell them they are to read the book, and as they are reading, fill out the data chart. In their reading, they will be looking for facts about World War II, changes in the United States during World War II, job opportunities for women during the war, and benefits for women then and now. Students should document the page number in the book where they located each fact for their chart.[1]

When data charts are completed, discuss findings with students. Have them respond to the following questions:

▶ How did life in the United States change during World War II?
▶ How did these changes compare to changes in Europe?
▶ How did the economy change in the United States?
▶ What job opportunities were open to women during the war?
▶ How did the economy benefit from working women?
▶ What might have happened to the economy if women had been unwilling or unable to work?
▶ How did the job opportunities for women change after the war ended?
▶ How do you think women felt about these changes?
▶ What benefits did women experience then? Now?
▶ How have career opportunities for women changed since World War II?

Women and World War II
Data Chart

Facts about World War II	Changes in the U.S. During the War	Job Opportunities for Women	Benefits for Women Then and Now

Have students use the information from their charts in creative writing. Students may choose to:

- ▶ Write a letter from a working woman to her husband who is serving in the military
- ▶ Write a letter from a man serving in the military to his working wife
- ▶ Write a diary entry of a working woman
- ▶ Write a diary entry of a woman who has just been laid off because the war is over

Ask students to share their writing in small groups.

Note

1. Modified from Patricia A. Antonacci and Catherine M. O'Callaghan, *A Handbook for Literacy: Instructional and Assessment Strategies K-8* (New York: Pearson, 2006).

COMPARE AND CONTRAST: USING VENN DIAGRAMS TO ANALYZE BOOKS AND MOVIES

Aleutian Sparrow **by Karen Hesse. (New York: Margaret K. Elderry Books, 2003).**

Genre: Historical fiction

Book Summary

It is World War II, and Vera lives with her mother in the Aleutian Islands off the coast of Alaska. The Japanese bomb Unalaska Island and capture and occupy the islands of Kiska and Attu. Although Vera, her mother, and her friends and neighbors have done nothing wrong, they are forced to leave their homes and enter internment camps in the southern part of Alaska, near Ketchikan. For three years they must live with no heat, running water, medical care, adequate food, or toilet facilities.

Vera and her family learn of a camp close by for German prisoners of war. They have cots, blankets, an infirmary, and good food to eat. No one at the internment camp understands why the Aleut, who are American citizens, are forced to live in squalid conditions. There is no work in the camp for Vera's mother, so she walks the eight miles into Ketchikan to find work. Many become sick and die, including Vera's good friend, Pari.

When the war is over and they are finally allowed to return home, Vera finds that her home is ruined. The American soldiers have shattered windows, broken possessions, and stolen keepsakes. Their fishing grounds are polluted, making the clams and mussels inedible. The churches have been looted, and priceless relics from Russia are gone. Vera and her family must find a way to begin again.

Social Studies Standards
❶ CULTURE
Ⅵ POWER, AUTHORITY, AND GOVERNANCE

Performance Expectations
❶ CULTURE
a. Compare similarities and differences in the ways groups, societies, and cultures meet human needs and concerns.

Ⅵ POWER, AUTHORITY, AND GOVERNANCE
h. Explain and apply concepts such as power, role, status, justice, and influence to the examination of persistent issues and social problems.

Language Arts Skills
Reading, listening, speaking, viewing

Materials
- ▶ Multiple copies of *Aleutian Sparrow* by Karen Hesse
- ▶ DVD: "Aleut Story"
- ▶ Venn diagrams (one per student)
- ▶ Internet access

Procedures

Ask students to name the places that were bombed by the Japanese during World War II. Mention the Aleutian Islands if students have not named them. Help students find the Aleutian Islands on a map of Alaska. Introduce the book and tell students that the facts in the story are true, but the characters are fictional. Discuss the unrhymed verse that Karen Hesse uses in her writing.

Have students read the book independently. Ask students to discuss the following questions:

- ▶ Were you aware that the Aleutians were sent to internment camps during World War II?
- ▶ Who held the power in this story? Explain.
- ▶ How should the United States use its power?
- ▶ What could the United States government have done differently to protect the Aleutians during the war?
- ▶ Describe the status and power of the Aleutians.
- ▶ How is the Aleutian culture different from other cultures with which you are familiar?
- ▶ How does the location of the Aleutian Islands contribute to their culture?
- ▶ Did the Aleutians ever receive justice for their losses during World War II?

Allow students to review the Aleutian World War II National Historic Area website at www.ounalashka.com. Have students discuss what the American government has done to make up for Aleutian losses during World War II.

Have students view the Aleut Story, a documentary that can be purchased at www.visionmaker.org/aleut_h.html. A teacher's guide and historic documents can be found at www.aleutstory.tv.

Venn Diagram

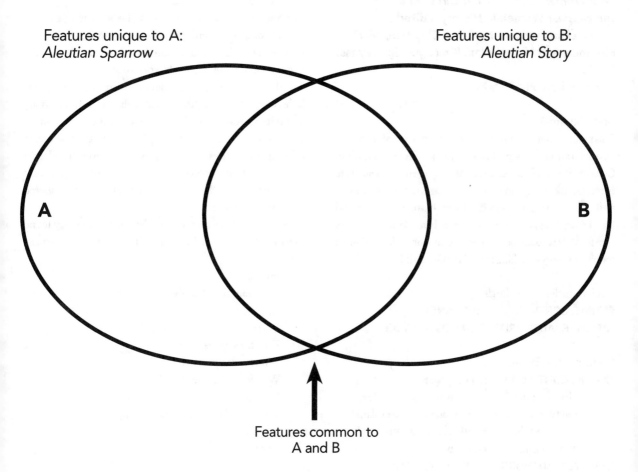

Features unique to A:
Aleutian Sparrow

Features unique to B:
Aleutian Story

A

B

Features common to
A and B

Give each student a Venn diagram. Have students compare and contrast Aleutian Sparrow with the Aleut Story. When they are finished, have them discuss ways the book and movie are alike and different. Have students discuss whether they believe the details and descriptions in the book are true.

COOL WOMEN IN HISTORY: COMPOSING BIOPOEMS

***Cool Women: The Thinking Girl's Guide to the Hippest Women in History*, edited by Pam Nelson, written by Dawn Chipman, Mari Florence, and Naomi Wax. (Chicago: Girl's Press, 1998).**
Genre: Biography, Fiction

Book Summary

This book is a compilation of real women and fictional characters, all of who are inspirational figures in history. From Nellie Bly to Calamity Jane to Nancy Drew, all of the women represented are heroines, risk takers, and leaders. Two pages of brightly colored, well-illustrated text are included for each woman. Quotes and little known facts are incorporated, and there is contact information for girls who might be interested in more information on topics from movie making to the Jane Goodall Institute.

Social Studies Standards
Ⓘ **TIME, CONTINUITY, AND CHANGE**
Ⓥ **POWER, AUTHORITY, AND GOVERNANCE**

Performance Expectations
Ⓘ **TIME, CONTINUITY, AND CHANGE**
b. Identify and use key concepts such as chronology, causality, change, conflict, and complexity to explain, analyze, and show connections among patterns of historical change and continuity.

Ⓥ **POWER, AUTHORITY, AND GOVERNANCE**
a. Examine persistent issues involving the rights, roles, and status of the individual in relation to the general welfare.

Language Arts Skills
Listening, reading, writing

Materials
▶ One copy of *Cool Women: The Thinking Girl's Guide to the Hippest Women in History* edited by Pam Nelson, written by Dawn Chipman, Mari Florence, and Naomi Wax
▶ Paper and pencils
▶ Library resources and the Internet

Procedures
Read excerpts aloud from the text on well-known or little-known women, or give students an opportunity to read selections independently. Choose a woman that you would like students to know more about, such as Harriet Tubman.

Allow students opportunities to research the woman you have chosen in more depth. Encourage them to use both library and Internet resources. Have students focus on the woman's accomplishments, skills, and conflicts, as well as her ability to effect change. For example, they might discover that Harriet Tubman was an undercover spy for the North during the ", she was referred to as "Black Moses," and slave owners offered $40,000 for her arrest.

As a class, have students use the information they found to write a biopoem on this woman. The following format can be used:

> First name
> Four traits that describe the character
> Relative of
> Lover of (three things or people)
> Who feels (three items)
> Who needs (three items)
> Who fears (three items)
> Who gives (three items)
> Who would like to see (three items)
> Resident of
> Last name

This format was used to compose this sample biopoem on Harriet Tubman.

> Harriet
> Adventurer, warrior, Black Moses, General
> Mother of freedom
> Lover of risk, black Americans, what's right
> Who feels determined, courageous, clever
> Who needs money for schools, help for the sick, homes for the aged
> Who fears no person, no place, no thing
> Who gives her mind, her body, her spirit
> Who would like to see all that is right, all that is good, freedom for all

Resident of the Harriet Tubman Home for the Aged
and Indigent Colored People
Tubman

Have each student choose another woman from the book. Encourage them to find out more information on this woman through library and Internet resources. Students should take notes on the woman's accomplishments, family, passions, skills, personality characteristics, and ability to effect change.

Ask each student to write a biopoem on the woman they have chosen. Encourage them to follow the correct format, use information from their research, and focus on creativity and word choice. After students have finished writing, allow them to share their drafts with classmates and make revisions based on peer feedback.

Post biopoems and pictures or drawings of the women to create a bulletin board.

Ask students to consider and discuss the following questions:

▶ What makes these women stand out in history?
▶ What qualities do they share?
▶ How are our lives different because of the work they did?
▶ What qualities does an individual need in order to bring about change?
▶ Do you see any of these qualities in yourself? Why or why not?

COMMUNITY-BASED RESEARCH: DISCOVERING LOCAL WOMEN IN HISTORY

Girls: A History of Growing Up Female in America by Penny Colman. (New York: Scholastic, 2000).
Genre: Nonfiction and biography

Book Summary
Girls: A History of Growing Up Female in America is a comprehensive account of what it has been like to grow up as a girl in America. Penny Colman begins with a chapter on understanding gender, with a summary of why boy babies have been favored throughout history. She then develops a chronology of events and stories, beginning with immigration and continuing through the Colonial period and into the nineteenth and twentieth centuries. Colman uses books, magazines, paintings, photographs, diaries, letters, advertisements, and song lyrics to discover all that girls have experienced. Stories of individual women from diverse backgrounds, along with an abundance of drawings and photographs, provide readers with a humanistic view of history not typically found in history textbooks.

Social Studies Standards
Ⓘ TIME, CONTINUITY, AND CHANGE
Ⓥ POWER, AUTHORITY, AND GOVERNANCE
Ⓧ CIVIC IDEALS AND PRACTICES

Performance Expectations
Ⓘ **TIME, CONTINUITY, AND CHANGE**
   b. Identify and use key concepts such as chronology, causality, change, conflict, and complexity to explain, analyze, and show connections among patterns of historical change and continuity.
Ⓥ **POWER, AUTHORITY, AND GOVERNANCE**
   a. Examine persistent issues involving the rights, roles, and status of the individual in relation to the general welfare.
Ⓧ **CIVIC IDEALS AND PRACTICES**
   a. Examine the origins and continuing influence of key ideals of the democratic republican form of government, such as individual human dignity, liberty, justice, equality, and the rule of law.

Language Arts Skills
Reading, writing, speaking, visually representing

Materials
▶ Multiple copies of *Girls: A History of Growing Up Female in America* by Penny Colman
▶ Library and Internet resources
▶ Butcher paper
▶ Markers and colored pencils

Procedures
Present concepts in Chapter One, "It's a Girl!," as an introduction to a study of the history of growing up female. Discuss the biological and environmental issues related to gender and how children throughout history have learned what it means to be a boy or a girl. Cite examples and childhood memories, such as those of Hilda Satt Polacheck and Frances Willard.

Divide students into small groups. Have each group read and discuss one of the nine remaining chapters. Give each group a long sheet of butcher paper and ask them to use the events in their chapter to make a timeline, extending the entire length of the sheet of paper. Students can use words, pictures, and photographs on their timeline to represent the events in their chapter. Beginning with the timeline for chapter two, "By Land and By Sea: How Girls Came to America," have students hang the timelines on the wall in chronological order, so they are connected into one long timeline. Give each group an opportunity to summarize the events and stories in their chapter.

Suggest to students that the timeline might be more meaningful and interesting if they added the history of women in their community and state. Discuss research methods and have students brainstorm sources of information about local women's history, such as the historical society, the courthouse, the military, the library, and teachers' organizations. Explain interviewing strategies and suggest sources of historical interview data, such as retired teachers and individuals who are constructing their family tree.

Have students brainstorm themes in women's history they are interested in learning about. For example, students might be interested in researching topics such as

▶ Famous women in their state and community

- ▶ Women in sports
- ▶ Immigration and its impact on women
- ▶ Women's rights
- ▶ Schooling for girls and young women
- ▶ Career opportunities
- ▶ Women in the military
- ▶ Women in government

Allow each of the original groups to choose one of the themes to research. Each group should discuss research methods, create interview questions, and coordinate their action plan. For example, the group that is researching schooling might choose to look at old maps to see where schools were located, determine how many girls graduated from high school during various periods in history, interview retired teachers to find out what teaching was like, and research the education of females at local colleges.

As students learn information from their research and interviews, have them place names, places, and events on the timeline. When research is complete, ask students to explain their additions to the timeline.

Have each research group choose the one person or event they found most interesting. Ask each group to design a creative method of sharing this person or event with the class. Groups can choose to perform a skit, conduct a simulated interview, write and perform a song, create an exhibit of artifacts, or film a video. Encourage students to work cooperatively and think creatively. Give each group an opportunity to perform for the class.

ADDITIONAL YOUNG ADULT LITERATURE TITLES FOR THE MIDDLE SCHOOL GRADES

Mary Jane Auch. *Journey to Nowhere* (New York: Yearling, 1998).

Eleven-year-old Mem and her family move from Connecticut to New York in 1815. Their journey is treacherous, and the story gives readers a good view of everyday life in the early 1800s.

Mary Jane Auch. *Frozen Summer* (New York: Yearling, 2000).

In the sequel to *Journey to Nowhere* (Yearling, 1998), the Nye family has moved to New York, and a very cold summer has caused farming to be poor. Mem's mother has had a new baby and is depressed, and Mem has had to give up her dream of an education to help at home.

Mary Jane Auch. *The Road to Home* (New York: Yearling, 2002).

This book is the sequel to *Journey to Nowhere* (1997) and *Frozen Summer* (1998). Thirteen-year-old Mem's mother has died, and she is left in charge of her two siblings while their father goes to work on the Erie Canal.

Karen Blumenthal. Let *Me Play: The Story of Title IX: The Law that Changed the Future of Girls in America* (New York: Atheneum, 2005).

This book provides the history of Title IX and glimpses into what life was like for female athletes before it was passed. Statistics, archival photographs, cartoons, and player profiles make this topic an interesting one for adolescent readers.

Muriel Branch. *Pennies to Dollars: The Story of Maggie Lena Walker* (New Haven, CT: Linnet, 1997).

Maggie Walker was the daughter of a former slave and a white abolitionist. She was the founder of the first African American-owned bank in the United States and was a highly successful businesswoman.

Marian Hale. *The Truth about Sparrows* (New York: Henry Holt, 2004).

During the Depression, Sadie must leave her home in dust bowl Missouri to live in a one-room, tar-paper shack in coastal Texas. This story tells about the myriad of ways that families were affected economically and socially during the Depression era.

Karen Hesse. *A Time of Angels* (New York: Hyperion, 1995).

This novel recounts the story of Hannah, who was separated from her parents during World War I. She moves in with her aunt in Boston, but the family is again torn apart by the influenza epidemic. This book was an International Reading Association Young Adults' Choice for 1997.

Dorothy and Thomas Hoobler. *Real American Girls Tell Their Own Stories* (New York: Atheneum, 1999).

This book shares the real diaries of girls who lived across two centuries. The girls who are profiled come from very different backgrounds, and readers are able to discover how things have changed for girls over time.

Martha Kendall. *Failure is Impossible: The History of American Women's Rights* (Minneapolis, MN: Lerner Publishing, 2001).

This text looks at the history of women's rights from early Colonial times to the present day. Dozens of notable women are highlighted, along with organizations such as the League of Women Voters and the Women's Christian Temperance Union.

Laurie Lawlor. *Helen Keller: Rebellious Spirit* (New York: Holiday House, 2001).

This biography examines issues in Helen Keller's life that are typically not addressed, such as her finances and controversial Socialism. Helen's adventures in Broadway and Hollywood are included, along with her attempts to support herself during World War II.

Wendy Lawton. *Courage to Run: A Story Based on the Life of Harriet Tubman* (Chicago: Moody Press, 2002).

This book describes the inspirational life and courageous actions of Harriet Tubman. Written from a Christian perspective, the author tells of Harriet's unfailing hope and faith in God.

Joyce McDonald. *Devil On My Heels* (New York: Random House, 2004).

This novel is set in Florida in the 1950s, when racism and the activity of the Ku Klux Klan were rampant. Dove, age 15, and her peers confront Klansmen.

Joanne Oppenheim. *Dear Miss Breed* (New York: Scholastic, 2006).

The author tells the story of children who were interned in Japanese-American prison camps during World War II and the public librarian who sent them letters and care packages. The letters sent to and from these children are the foundation of the book, along with archival photographs and quotations.

Ann Rinaldi. *Sarah's Ground* (New York: Simon and Schuster, 2004).

Eighteen-year-old Sarah Tracy travels from her home in New York state to Mount Vernon to act as overseer. During the Civil War, Sarah uses her intelligence to influence President Lincoln to keep Mount Vernon on neutral ground.

Mary Ann Rodman. *Yankee Girl* (New York: Farrar, Straus, and Giroux Books, 2004).

This novel takes place in Mississippi in 1964. Alice's FBI father must protect African Americans who are registering to vote. The Ku Klux Klan is burning churches, civil rights leaders have been murdered, and now a black girl enters Alice's class as a result of mandatory integration.

Mindy Warshaw Skolsky. *Love from Your Friend, Hannah* (New York: Scholastic, 1998).

This work of fiction tells the story of Hannah, whose best friend moves away during the Depression and doesn't bother to write to her. Instead, Hannah writes letters to President Franklin D. Roosevelt, First Lady Eleanor Roosevelt, and the President's secretary, who all return her correspondence.

Catherine Thimmesh. *Madam President: The Extraordinary, True (and Evolving) Story of Women in Politics* (Boston: Houghton Mifflin, 2004).

This book provides sketches of women involved in politics in America and across the world. Timelines, source materials, quotes, and cartoons supplement historical information on each subject.

CHAPTER FIVE

Teaching Women's History in the High School Grades

By the time students enter high school, they have some knowledge of major events, time periods, and famous people in history. However, if they were taught through a textbook approach, students may have limited knowledge of women's history, outside of facts learned through isolated discussions during Women's History Month. Beyond knowing facts about history, high school students should be able to demonstrate historical thinking and understanding. They need opportunities to demonstrate what they have learned and to apply their knowledge to understand both the past and the present.

According to the National Standards for History, the essence of history is "a process of reasoning based on evidence from the past."[1] Students must be able to interpret cause and effect relationships, analyze historical findings, and conduct research, so that knowledge from the past can be used to solve contemporary problems. By the high school grades, the majority of students are able to think abstractly and hypothetically. At this level, students are able to consider ambiguities, detect bias, and reveal the political basis of events in United States history, making for excellent classroom discussions and debates.

Whether learning history through textbooks or trade books, students must use critical literacy to interpret historical knowledge. They must consider whose knowledge is in print, what perspectives are included and whose are missing, and who the knowledge will benefit. They must determine if the winners of history are the only ones that are documented, silencing voices of women and minorities. How are we to develop critical literacy in adolescents? Classrooms must be safe places for open discussion, such that students feel safe to express their opinions and ideas, especially when the topics are controversial. There must be dialogues, debates, and discussions, so adolescents have chances to form opinions and perspectives on social, historical, and political issues. Constructivist learning opportunities must be a routine part of classroom instruction, so students can be actively involved in demonstrating their knowledge of history.[2]

At this point in students' education, the big ideas of history are more important than the names, dates, and places. Historical fiction and biographies, both at the young adult and adult levels, allow high school students to explore big ideas, such as

prejudice and oppression, by experiencing the lives of men and women of the past. Teachers can use critical elements and plots in books to help students confront these big ideas, while inviting them to consider ways they can use the past to better the present and future.

In this chapter, students discover the Founding Mothers of our nation, working conditions for women during the height of immigration, the perils of school integration, and stories of women involved in the rescue of 9/11 victims. They become involved in research, writing, artistic presentation, and community change. Most importantly, students learn lessons from the past that they can use to better their own future and the future of our nation. 🖼

Notes

1. National Center for History in the Schools. *National Standards for History* (Los Angeles, CA: Author, 1996). The citation is on page 49.
2. Steven Wolk. "Teaching for Critical Literacy in Social Studies," *The Social Studies* (2003):101.

THE WOMEN WHO RAISED OUR NATION: PARTICIPATING IN RESEARCH DISCUSSIONS

Founding Mothers: The Women Who Raised Our Nation **by Cokie Roberts. (New York: Harper, 2005).**
Genre: Biography

Book Summary

This book contains stories of the women who influenced the Founding Fathers of this nation. Many of the stories come from letters that were written by them and to them. The stories take place before, during, and after the time the Declaration of Independence was signed and tell of the women's role in the Revolution. Many quotes from Founding Fathers and Mothers are included throughout the stories, and, although the language in the letters has been modernized for ease in reading, the historical nature of the conversations is evident.

Many of the women whose stories are told here are well known. However, even though women such as Abigail Adams and Martha Washington are represented in history textbooks, the stories of their influence and contributions during the Revolution are not widely known. For example, John Adams, husband to Abigail, was a member of the Continental Congress and away from home months out of the year. That left Abigail to tend to their many children, run the farm, and watch the city of Boston prepare for war. She was considered a "feisty female" who always supported the weak. She was not afraid to tell her husband her thoughts on women's rights, slavery, or the fight for independence. In one letter to John, she asked that he "Remember the ladies and be more generous and favorable to them than your ancestors." These famous words are a reminder that during this period in history, men legally owned their wives under English law.

In addition to women who had close relationships with the Founding Fathers, there are stories of women who dressed as men to participate in battle, female spies who had strong influence on the outcome of the war, and women such as Molly Pitcher, who did not bother to dress like a man in order to enter the battlefield. For many, this book provides the first opportunity to read the words and hear the thoughts and opinions of women who lived and influenced this period in history.

Social Studies Standards
TIME, CONTINUITY, AND CHANGE
CIVIC IDEALS AND PRACTICES

Performance Expectations
TIME, CONTINUITY, AND CHANGE

d. Systematically employ processes of critical historical inquiry to reconstruct and reinterpret the past, such as using a variety of sources and checking their credibility, validating and weighing evidence for claims, and searching for causality.

CIVIC IDEALS AND PRACTICES

a. Explain the origins and interpret the continuing influence of key ideals of the democratic republican form of government, such as individual human dignity, liberty, justice, equality, and the rule of law

Language Arts Skills
Reading, writing, speaking, listening

Materials
▶ Multiple copies of *Founding Mothers: The Women Who Raised Our Nation* by Cokie Roberts
▶ Library and Internet Resources

Procedures
Ask students to name women who influenced the fight for independence and the formation of our nation. List names on the chalkboard and have students explain their roles and contributions.

Have students read all of the text or key chapters in the text. Have them add additional names to the list on the chalkboard and then consider the following questions:

▶ In what ways did women influence the Founding Fathers?
▶ What were their positions on key issues such as women's rights, slavery, and independence?
▶ What ideals (such as equality, liberty, and justice) were written into the Declaration of Independence, but not made available to women? Why?
▶ What are your opinions on the irony of women fighting

for independence for their country, when they themselves could not claim it?

▶ What influence did these women have on present day laws and policies?

▶ Why do you think stories of these women are not typically included in American history textbooks?

Have students participate in small group research discussions related to topics and themes in the text. For example, students may wish to investigate themes such as:

▶ Women's rights from the time of the Declaration of Independence to the present

▶ The influence of First Ladies on the history of our nation and its people

▶ The education of women from the time of our independence to the present

▶ Women spies and soldiers of the American Revolution

▶ The Daughters of Liberty

Have students choose the topic they would like to research and form small groups with other students who are interested in the same topic. (Four or five students per group usually works best.) Ask students to break their topic into subtopics. For example, students who are investigating the education of women might research subtopics such as:

▶ Dame schools and one-room school houses and girls' experiences there

▶ The first colleges and universities to accept women and their experiences there

▶ Title IX and its impact on the education of girls and women

▶ Gender bias and its effects on girls and women

Have the students in each group select a subtopic and formulate that subtopic into a research question. For example, in the Title IX group, one question might read, "What is Title IX, and what impact has it had on the education of girls and women?" After all students have research questions, they must find at least five sources to answer their question. Students may use books, journals, newspapers, Internet resources, or personal interviews. Using the information in their five sources, students create a one-page research discussion outline of information they would like to share with the other members of their small group. Discussion questions should be embedded in the outline so each student can involve other group members in a discussion of their topic. (See sample research discussion outline on page 92.) Discuss the outline format and citation style with students. Each student is to make copies of her or his one-page research discussion outline for each member of the small group.

On the day(s) of the research discussions, groups sit together in a circle and everyone in the group has a copy of all the research discussion outlines. Ask students to decide the order of presentation, and give each student 15 minutes to lead their discussion. Encourage students to know their topic well enough to be able to lead their discussion with few, if any, notes in front of them. Their outline should be their guide, and they should use their discussion questions to foster discussion and exchange of opinions and information on their research question.

When the first student in each group has finished his or her discussion, call time and have the second discussion leader begin. Continue until all students have led their 15-minute discussion.

When the members of each small group have led their discussions, begin regrouping. Have students form new groups in which there is now one member of each of the original groups. In these new groups, students take turns leading a discussion using all of the information they know about their topic -- information they researched as well as information they learned from their original group members. Again, encourage students to foster discussion and share opinions.

Students turn in their research discussion outlines and bibliographies.

Sample Research Discussion Outline

I.   Gender Bias and Its Effects on Girls and Women

    A.   The History of Gender Bias

    B.   The Research of Sadker and Sadker (see p. 8, note 11)

    C.   The Work of the American Association of University Women

    D.   Title IX and Other Legislation

Discussion Question: Do you think our legislators have done enough to rid our schools of gender bias? Why or why not?

II.   Gender Bias and Elementary Age Students

    A.   Learning to Read

    B.   Teacher/Student Interactions

    C.   Playground Experiences

Discussion Question: When you were young, what interactions and experiences did you have to foster your gender role development?

III.   Gender Bias and Secondary Age Students

    A.   Higher-Level Math, Science, and Computer Science

    B.   SAT Scores

    C.   Scholarships

Discussion Question: Does bias continue to be present in any aspect of your high school experience? How?

IV.   Gender Bias in College

    A.   A Comparison of Majors among Males and Females

    B.   Experiences in College Courses

Discussion Question: Why do we continue to have more girls majoring in nursing and elementary education and more boys majoring in engineering and computer science?

V.   Gender Bias in the Workplace

    A.   Sexual Harassment

    B.   The Glass Ceiling

    C.   Employment Choices and Opportunities

Discussion Question: What do you think is the major reason why only a very small percentage of the CEOs of major companies are women?

GIVING VOICES TO THE SILENCED: WRITING INTERIOR MONOLOGUES

The Face of Our Past: Images of Black Women from Colonial America to the Present, edited by Kathleen Thompson and Hilary Mac Austin. (Bloomington, IN: Indiana University Press, 1999).
Genre: Pictorial nonfiction

Book Summary

This book presents photographs and drawings of African American women throughout history. With only brief captions, these images tell the stories of slaves, teachers, Girl Scouts, athletes, beauty pageant contestants, tenant farmers, and civil rights activists. Notable women, such as Shirley Chisholm, Sojourner Truth, and Wilma Rudolph, are incorporated into this volume, but the majority of photographs are of women who hold no notoriety. Many of them remain unnamed.

These photographs bring about varying emotions. Elation, hope, and loneliness are all portrayed, and some of the images are disturbing. Lynchings and beatings were fairly common well into the 1900s. In addition to photographs, there are quotations from both famous and little-known black women throughout history. Their words highlight the visual images and provide readers with historical context.

Social Studies Standards
⊗ CIVIC IDEALS AND PRACTICES

Performance Expectations

a. Explain the origins and interpret the continuing influence of key ideals of the democratic republican form of government, such as individual human dignity, liberty, justice, equality, and the rule of law.

e. Analyze and evaluate the influence of various forms of citizen action on public policy

Language Arts Skills
Reading, viewing, speaking, listening, writing

Materials
▶ Multiple copies of *The Face of Our Past: Images of Black Women from Colonial America to the Present*, edited by Kathleen Thompson and Hilary Mac Austin

Procedures

Give students an opportunity to view the photographs and read the captions and quotes in the book. Viewing should not be hurried. Students should have sufficient time to contemplate the faces and consider the lives and experiences of these women. Have students consider the following questions:

▶ How is human dignity represented in these images?
▶ How are equality and inequality represented?
▶ How are justice and injustice and the laws of our land represented?
▶ What did these women do to fight the inequalities and injustices in our nation?
▶ What changes have been made in our society as a result of their battles?
▶ What do you think of when you look at their faces? What comes to mind?
▶ Have you ever considered what they might have been thinking when the photographs were taken?

Ask each student to select three photographs from the book. For each photograph, students will write interior monologues for the woman or women represented. Interior monologues are the imagined thoughts of a person at a specific point in history. Explain to students that interior monologues give voice to people whose voices have been silenced by injustices.[1] Discuss the injustices these women have experienced and the ways their voices have been silenced.

After students have completed their writing, have them form small groups. In each group, students will take turns sharing the photographs they have chosen and the interior monologue for each image. Each student should be encouraged to explain why they believe the women would have those particular thoughts. After all students have shared, ask them to consider how the lives of these women and our nation's history might have been different if their thoughts had been voiced.

Note

1. Modified from L. Christensen and B. Bigelow, "Promoting Social Imagination through Interior Monologues," in B. Bigelow (ed.), *Rethinking Our Classrooms: Teaching for Equity and Justice*, Vol. 1 (Milwaukee, WI: Rethinking Schools, 1994).

FOR THE LOVE OF POETRY: EXPERIENCING THE POEMS OF PHILLIS WHEATLEY

Hang a Thousand Trees with Ribbons: The Story of Phillis Wheatley by Ann Rinaldi. (New York: Scholastic, 1996).

Genre: Historical fiction

Book Summary

As a young girl, Keziah lived with her family on the Grain Coast near the River Senegal in Africa. In 1761, Her uncle sold Keziah, her mother, and her best friend to slave traders and they sailed to America. During the voyage, her mother was thrown overboard. Keziah and her friend arrived in Massachusetts in a pen. Keziah was sold to John Wheatley and was renamed "Phillis," after the boat she arrived on.

Phillis came to live with Mr. and Mrs. Wheatley, Mary, and Nathaniel. Although she was initially a servant for Mary, Mary mistreated her. Phillis was taken away from Mary and was then well cared for by the Wheatley family. Nathanial taught her to read and write, during a time when slaves were typically uneducated. The family was excited to discover that Phillis was very intelligent, and she began studying Latin, Greek, and the classics. When Phillis was thirteen, she began writing poetry. The Wheatley's were overwhelmed at her talent, because it was widely believed that Africans were unable to learn.

As her poetry writing continued, Phillis learned that Mr. and Mrs. Wheatley wanted to have a book of her poems published. However, no publishers would agree to publish her work because they felt their readers would not believe that a "nigra" girl could be this gifted. Phillis went before a review board, which included John Hancock and the governor of Massachusetts, to answer questions about her poetry and her knowledge of history and literature. She passed the review with flying colors and traveled with Nathaniel to London in search of a publisher. While there, she met Benjamin Franklin and secured a publisher. Once home, Phillis requested freedom, which she was granted, and became the first published black poet.

Social Studies Standards
⊕ TIME, CONTINUITY, AND CHANGE

Performance Expectation

d. Systematically employ processes of critical historical inquiry to reconstruct and reinterpret the past, such as using a variety of sources and checking their credibility, validating and weighing evidence for claims, and searching for causality.

Language Arts Skills

Reading, speaking, listening, visually representing

Materials

- ▶ Multiple copies of *Hang a Thousand Trees with Ribbons: The Story of Phillis Wheatley* by Ann Rinaldi
- ▶ Internet access
- ▶ Art paper, markers, colored pencils, pastels, paints

Procedures

Access www.poemhunter.com and select one of the 55 poems of Phillis Wheatley. Read the poem aloud to students and discuss its theme and author. Inform students that the poem was written by the first African American author, while she was a slave in the 1700s.

Have students read *Hang a Thousand Trees with Ribbons: The Story of Phillis Wheatley* independently. Ask them to consider the following questions:

- ▶ What did you learn about slavery that you didn't know before reading this book?
- ▶ What, if anything, disturbed you about this story? Why?
- ▶ What were some of the stereotypes about African Americans during the time this story took place?
- ▶ What do you think would have happened to Phillis and her poetry if she had not been "purchased" by John Wheatley?

Have students access www.poemhunter.com and select one of Phillis Wheatley's poems. Give them an opportunity to practice reading their selection, and then have volunteers read their poems aloud. Students can also participate in choral speaking as all the students in the class take turns reading different parts of the same poem. Discuss the theme of each poem and what can be learned about the historical period and the author's life from the content of the poems.

Provide students with art paper and materials. Have them illustrate the poem they selected. As they plan their design, encourage students to consider the theme of the poem, the historical context, and the author's life. In small groups, have students share their poems and illustrations, providing explanations for their designs.

SEND-A-PROBLEM: INVOLVING STUDENTS IN SMALL GROUP PROBLEM-SOLVING

Forbidden Schoolhouse: The True and Dramatic Story of Prudence Crandall and Her Students by Suzanne Jurmain. (Boston: Houghton Mifflin, 2005).
Genre: Biography

Book Summary

The Forbidden Schoolhouse: The True and Dramatic Story of Prudence Crandall and Her Students is the story of one woman's attempt to open a school for African American girls during a period in history when it was illegal to educate black students in many states. Prudence Crandall successfully operated a boarding school for white girls, until she was approached by an African American girl seeking admission. Ms. Crandall allowed the girl to enroll, enraging parents and the community. She refused to back down, as she truly wanted to help girls who were receiving no education.

With assistance from William Lloyd Garrison (an abolitionist and newspaper editor) and Arthur Tappan (a wealthy New York businessman), Crandall finally decided to open a school for African-American girls in Canterbury, Connecticut. She had many adversaries, and soon shopkeepers boycotted her, and she was placed in jail. This text, rich with photographs and other primary documents, ends with the civil rights movement that took place long after Crandall's death. The appendix includes the names and descriptions of the African American girls who attended the school and facts on the friends and adversaries who were involved in Crandall's struggles.

Social Studies Standards
Ⓘ TIME, CONTINUITY, AND CHANGE
Ⓥ POWER, AUTHORITY, AND GOVERNANCE
Ⓧ CIVIC IDEALS AND PRACTICES

Performance Expectations
Ⓘ TIME, CONTINUITY, AND CHANGE
b. Apply key concepts such as time, chronology, causality, change, conflict, and complexity to explain, analyze, and show connections among patterns of historical change and continuity.

Ⓥ POWER, AUTHORITY, AND GOVERNANCE
h. Explain and apply ideas, theories, and modes of inquiry drawn from political science to the examination of persistent issues and social problems.

Ⓧ CIVIC IDEALS AND PRACTICES
e. Analyze and evaluate the influence of various forms of citizen action on public policy

Language Arts Skills
Reading, Speaking, Writing, Listening

Materials
► One copy of *Forbidden Schoolhouse: The True and Dramatic Story of Prudence Crandall and Her Students* by Suzanne Jurmain
► Three 4 x 9" envelopes
► Six index cards

Procedures

Allow students opportunities to read *Forbidden Schoolhouse: The True and Dramatic Story of Prudence Crandall and Her Students*. You may choose to implement the "read-a-book-an-hour" strategy.[1] Engage students in a discussion of the following questions:

► Why do you think Prudence Crandall felt so strongly about the education of African American girls?
► What skills and qualities did Prudence possess to help her overcome problems and adversaries?
► How do individuals develop these types of qualities and skills?

Involve students in a collaborative-learning strategy called Send-A-Problem.[2] Write one of the following problems related to the story on the outside of each of the three envelopes.

Problem #1: Prudence Crandall demonstrated throughout her lifetime what one person can do to advocate for and ease the burden of others. If more people today were involved in serving others, we would have a much stronger nation. Are there modern-day Prudence Crandalls? If so, who are they, and how are they making a difference? How can you, as adolescents, make a difference in the lives of others?

Problem #2: According to the Urban Institute (an economic and social policy research organization), in 2001 the high school graduation rate was 68 percent. However, 75 percent of Caucasians graduated, while only about 50 percent of African American and Hispanic students completed their education. Consider these statistics, and discuss the following: Do students have equal educational opportunities in the United States? What can schools do to increase graduation rates for minority students? What can students do to increase the graduation rates of their peers?

Problem #3: What has changed in the field of education since Prudence Crandall's time? What has remained the same? What do you think should be accomplished at the national and state levels to improve the education of all students in this country?

Divide the class into three groups and give each group an envelope and two index cards. Ask each group to discuss the problem on the outside of their envelope, brainstorm solutions or responses, reach consensus on the best solutions, write their solutions on one of the index cards, and place the card in the envelope.

When all groups are finished with their first problem, have students pass their envelope to another group and the process is repeated. These groups consider this new problem, add their index cards to the envelopes, and pass them on. The task of each final group is to review the solutions from the first two groups and determine which they believe is the best. They can add any suggestions they believe to be useful before reporting to the class on their analysis and decision.

Notes

1. See R. T. Vacca, "The Book an Hour Strategy," *Middle School Journal* 14 (1983): 17-19.
2. See E. Barkley, K. Cross, and C. Major. *Collaborative Learning Techniques: A Handbook for College Faculty* (San Francisco, CA: Jossey-Bass, 2005).

WHAT DOES THE FUTURE HOLD? WRITING EPILOGUES

Numbering the Bones **by Ann Rinaldi. (New York: Hyperion, 2002).**

Genre: Historical fiction

Book Summary

Eulinda was a slave girl on a plantation in Andersonville, Georgia, and a daughter of her master. Her little brother, Zeke, had been sold to slave traders, and her older brother, Neddy, had run off to join the Union army. When Neddy fled, he took with him a ruby ring that had been the cause of the sale of his brother. Nearby was Andersonville prison, home to thousands of Union soldiers from the Civil War. They were dying from starvation and disease. Eulinda soon learned that her brother Neddy was captive in the prison, and would surely die there if not rescued.

Eulinda got permission from her master to visit the prison and see if she could find Neddy. The prisoners she saw were half-dead men, ragged figures who were filthy and diseased. Although she didn't see him, she knew he was there. She implored her master to rescue him, but Neddy refused to leave prison and return to his life of slavery.

With the good work of President Lincoln, Eulinda soon became free. She returned to the prison many times to try and find her brother, who she knew had perished. In Neddy's grave, she found the ruby ring. Clara Barton came to Andersonville to help create a proper cemetery for the soldiers who died, and she and Eulinda soon became work partners and friends. Eulinda became Clara's secretary and was invited to travel with her to Washington, DC, where they would continue to work together. Eulinda gave Clara the ruby ring, to be used to support a new life for a black family.

Social Studies Standards
❶ TIME, CONTINUITY, AND CHANGE

Performance Expectations

d. Systematically employ processes of critical historical inquiry to reconstruct and reinterpret the past, such as using a variety of sources and checking their credibility, validating and weighing evidence for claims, and searching for causality.

Language Arts Skills
Reading, speaking, writing, listening

Materials
- ▶ Multiple copies of *Numbering the Bones* by Ann Rinaldi
- ▶ Library and Internet access

Procedures
Show students a ring (one with a red stone, if possible), and ask them to predict the significance of the ring to the story. Have students read the book independently, and have them respond to the following questions:

- ▶ How would you describe the character of Eulinda?
- ▶ How does she demonstrate strength and courage?
- ▶ What significance does the ring have in the story?
- ▶ Were you aware of Clara Barton's role at Andersonville Prison?
- ▶ How would you describe Clara Barton?

Ask students to write an epilogue to *Numbering the Bones*. In preparation for their writing, have them consider:

- ▶ What Clara is doing ten years later
- ▶ What Eulinda is doing ten years later
- ▶ What life is like for freed slaves ten years after the end of the Civil War
- ▶ What happened to the ring?

Although students are writing historical fiction, encourage them to keep the story within an accurate historical context. Have them use library and Internet resources to research Clara Barton and her work after the Civil War and the fate of freed slaves.

When students have completed first drafts, have them share their epilogues in small groups. Have peers give feedback on interest level, historical accuracy, and mechanics and sentence structure. Encourage students to make revisions based on peer feedback. Establish new groups, and have students share epilogues a second time. Ask them to compare and contrast characters, setting, and plot.

READ A BOOK IN AN HOUR: ASHES OF ROSES

***Ashes of Roses* by Mary Jane Auch. (New York: Laurel-Leaf, 2002).**

Genre: Historical fiction

Book Summary

Sixteen-year-old Rose Nolan emigrated from Ireland to America with her family. During inspection at Ellis Island, they discovered that baby Joseph had an eye infection and would not be permitted to enter the country. Rose's father decided to return Joseph to Ireland for a stay with his grandmother, while the rest of the family lived with Uncle Patrick in New York City. Rose, her mother, and her two sisters came to stay in a home where they were not welcome. Tensions ran high, and Ma Nolan had little money to spare.

Ma Nolen decided that she and her girls must return to Ireland. Rose and her younger sister, Maureen, wanted to stay in America and refused to board the ship. With the little money they had from selling their boarding tickets, they rented a room, and Rose began looking for work. She learned to sew and began working at the Triangle Shirtwaist Factory. Rose made friends quickly and enjoyed her work. Although Maureen was to be in school, she refused to go and also began working at the factory.

On March 25, 1911, Rose and Maureen were preparing to leave work for the day. Suddenly there was fire. The workers were locked in the building with no way to escape the flames. Many women jumped from the eighth and ninth floors to their death. Rose escaped by grabbing the elevator cable as the elevator went down for the last time. Although she thought Maureen had died in the fire, they were reunited later that day. One hundred and forty-six workers, mostly women, died in the famous Triangle Shirtwaist Factory fire.

Social Studies Standards
Ⓜ TIME, CONTINUITY, AND CHANGE
Ⓧ CIVIC IDEALS AND PRACTICES

Performance Expectations
Ⓜ TIME, CONTINUITY, AND CHANGE

d. Systematically employ processes of critical historical inquiry to reconstruct and reinterpret the past, such as using a variety of sources and checking their credibility, validating and weighing evidence for claims, and searching for causality.

Ⓧ CIVIC IDEALS AND PRACTICES

e. Analyze and evaluate the influence of various forms of citizen action on public policy.

i. Construct a policy statement and an action plan to achieve one or more goals related to an issue of public concern.

Language Arts Skills
Listening, reading, speaking, writing

Materials
▶ Multiple copies of *Ashes of Roses* by Mary Jane Auch
▶ Library and Internet resources

Procedures

In *Read a Book in an Hour*,[1] each student is responsible for reading only one chapter in a paperback book. This can be achieved in two ways. Paperback copies can be torn into chapters or, if enough copies are available, students can simply be given a book and assigned a chapter to read. There are 32 chapters in *Ashes of Roses*. Depending on the number of students in the class, the teacher can be assigned the first one or two chapters and the last one or two chapters, with students assigned the remaining chapters.

Read the first one or two chapters aloud. Have students predict what will happen in the next chapter and the remainder of the book. All students then begin reading their assigned chapters. In this book, the chapters are short and reading will go quickly. Have students put their chairs in a circle in the order of the book chapters. The student who read chapter two (or three) begins and briefly summarizes their chapter. That student also makes a prediction on what she or he thinks will happen in the next chapter. The next student summarizes and makes predictions and so on, until all students have summarized their chapters.

Read the last one or two chapters aloud.

Have students discuss the following:

- Is this story based on a true event in history?
- What do you know about the Triangle Shirtwaist Factory fire?
- How could we learn more?

Ask students to find out more about the Triangle Shirtwaist Factory fire and why it occurred. They can use books such as *The Triangle Fire* by Leon Stein,[2] websites such as Cornell University's (www.ilr.cornell.edu/trianglefire/), or newspaper accounts. Ask students to consider the following:

- Why were working conditions so poor for female immigrants?
- What did women do to improve working conditions?
- Did women have the same rights as men in other areas of life? Give some examples.
- What did women do to change public policies and laws?
- How do employment practices and salaries of men and women compare today?

In small groups, have students choose an issue of public concern. It can be an issue at the school, community, state, or national level. For example, students might be interested in changing a policy at the community level, such as no skateboarding being allowed on the sidewalks. Have each group research their concern and write a goal and an action plan to achieve that goal.

Give each group an opportunity to share their goal and action plan with the class. Ask peers to give feedback and suggestions to each group. Have students discuss the resources that would be necessary in order for each group to move forward with their action plan. If possible, have students carry out their action plans. Then, ask students to consider the following:

- How successful were you in making change? Why?
- Why is it so difficult to change public policy?
- What resources are needed in order for change to take place?

Notes

1. Adapted from R. T. Vacca, "The Book an Hour Strategy," *Middle School Journal* 14 (1983): 17-19.
2. Leon Stein, *The Triangle Fire* (Ithaca, NY: ILR Press, 2001).

WORDS OF WISDOM: ELEANOR ROOSEVELT AND THE WOMEN OF TODAY

The Wisdom of Eleanor Roosevelt edited by Donald Wigal. (New York: Citadel Press, 2003).

Our Eleanor: A Scrapbook Look at Eleanor Roosevelt's Remarkable Life by Candace Fleming. (New York: Atheneum, 2005).
Genre: Nonfiction, biography

Book Summaries
The Wisdom of Eleanor Roosevelt
Eleanor Roosevelt is considered one of the most influential women of the twentieth century. She was a humanitarian, a heroine, an advocate, an activist, and writer, and a leader. In 1958 she was chosen in a Gallup poll as the most admired American and was named "Woman of the Century" by the National Women's Hall of Fame. Mrs. Roosevelt lived during a time when women did not speak out on issues of public concern. However, she traveled the world representing her country and met with leaders such as the queen of England, Winston Churchill, and Gandhi.

This book is a compilation of 500 quotations in chronological order; passages from letters to her daughter, President Harry S. Truman and others; "My Day" newspaper columns; the Universal Declaration of Human Rights, of which she is the primary author; and Mrs. Roosevelt's obituary. The information included in the book comes from books, articles, newspaper articles, and letters written by Mrs. Roosevelt; and books and articles written about her.

Our Eleanor: A Scrapbook Look at Eleanor Roosevelt's Remarkable Life
Our Eleanor: A Scrapbook Look at Eleanor Roosevelt's Remarkable Life is replete with photographs, newspaper articles, letters, government documents, and other primary sources on the life of one of our most famous first ladies. The FBI files, magazine columns, and political cartoons in this volume make it an interesting text for young adult readers. Our Eleanor tells the story of Mrs. Roosevelt's life, interwoven with the history of the times. She lived through two world wars, the Great Depression, and a turbulent period in civil rights. The author describes Mrs. Roosevelt's work to ease poverty and advocate for civil rights, as well as her legacy as a first lady and representative to the United Nations.

Social Studies Standards
Ⓘⓥ INDIVIDUAL DEVELOPMENT AND IDENTITY
Ⓧ CIVIC IDEALS AND PRACTICES

Performance Expectations
Ⓘⓥ INDIVIDUAL DEVELOPMENT AND IDENTITY
g. Compare and evaluate the impact of stereotyping, conformity, acts of altruism, and other behaviors on individuals and groups.

Ⓧ CIVIC IDEALS AND PRACTICES
e. Analyze and evaluate the influence of various forms of citizen action on public policy.
f. Analyze a variety of public policies and issues from the perspective of formal and informal political actors.

Language Arts Skills
Reading, listening, speaking, writing, visually representing

Materials
▶ Multiple copies of *The Wisdom of Eleanor Roosevelt* edited by Donald Wigal.
▶ Multiple copies of *Our Eleanor: A Scrapbook Look at Eleanor Roosevelt's Remarkable Life* by Candace Fleming.
▶ Library and Internet resources
▶ Computer access and PowerPoint capability

Procedures
Read select quotes from both books, such as:
"For the young person the discovery of his own unsuspected capacity is an exciting, a liberating experience. We cannot deny that we have failed dismally to achieve this result of helping our young people to develop their maximum capacity." (Wigal, p. 91)

"The woman who dresses to suit her particular type, with only a moderate bowing acquaintance with fashion, comes out better than the woman who is a slave to the designer of the moment." (Wigal, p. 64)

"We have had, of course, a few failures among women who have taken office either because men have urged them to do so, or because they have followed in their husbands' footsteps. When a woman fails, it is much more serious than when a man fails, because the average person attributes the failure not to the individual, but to the fact that she is a woman." (Wigal, p. 26)

"One of the main destroyers of freedom is our attitude toward the colored race...We must face this problem and change our actions, or democracy will fade." (Fleming, p. 77)

"A woman can do any job a man can...and she deserves to be paid equally for doing it." (Fleming, p. 77)

Discuss each quote with students, encouraging them to offer their insights and opinions. Ask students to discuss whether each quote continues to have meaning in contemporary society.

Have students read the remainder of the books independently, noting any quotations that have special meaning for them. Have students discuss the following questions:

▶ What quotations did you find especially meaningful, and why?

▶ Does the wisdom of Eleanor Roosevelt continue to ring true in contemporary society? Why or why not?

▶ What were Mrs. Roosevelt's most notable accomplishments? Why?

▶ Why do you think she gave her life so unselfishly to help others?

▶ What personality characteristics can be attributed to Mrs. Roosevelt?

▶ Why did Harry S. Truman title her "The First Lady of the World"?

▶ What impact has the Declaration of Human Rights had on our global society?

▶ Why did Mrs. Roosevelt find the Declaration of Human Rights to be so important?

▶ How is Mrs. Roosevelt's obituary different from other obituaries you have read?

Have each student identify a contemporary woman who shares the same values, personality characteristics, and leadership qualities as Mrs. Roosevelt. Students can search magazines, newspapers, books, video clips, biographical databases, and Internet websites to make their selections. Ask each student to create and present a PowerPoint presentation to highlight this woman's accomplishments and personal attributes. Each presentation should make comparisons between the woman they have chosen and Mrs. Roosevelt.[1]

Note

1. G. Taylor. "Who's Who? Engaging Biography Study," *The Reading Teacher* 56 (2002/2003): 342-344.

DAISY BATES: A TIMELINE OF COURAGE

The Power of One: Daisy Bates and the Little Rock Nine by Judith Bloom Fradin and Dennis Brindell Fradin. (New York: Clarion, 2004).
Genre: Biography

Book Summary

Daisy Bates was born in rural Arkansas. She was raised by family friends after her mother was murdered and her father left and never returned. Like many southern towns in the early 1900s, Daisy's hometown was racially segregated, and she experienced many injustices. She began to hate white people. When the man who adopted her was dying, he told Daisy to hate the discrimination and insults, but not the people. He encouraged her to try and do something about the injustices that she and others experienced.

As a result of her adoptive father's words, Daisy Bates became one of the most courageous civil rights leaders of our time. She turned her hatred into action by co-publishing a widely read black newspaper, and she and her husband became two of the most influential journalists of their time. She became more directly involved in civil rights when, in 1952, she became president of the Arkansas chapter of the National Association for the Advancement of Colored People (NAACP).

Daisy Bates was perhaps best known for coordinating school integration efforts. In May of 1954, the United States Supreme Court declared that separate schools had no place in America. Many school districts were reticent, but by 1957 Daisy began meeting with nine African American high school students in preparation for the beginning of the new school year. President Eisenhower ordered federal guards to protect them, and as a result, the Little Rock schools were finally integrated.

Social Studies Standards
- **ⅠⅠ TIME, CONTINUITY, AND CHANGE**
- **ⅥⅠ POWER, AUTHORITY, AND GOVERNANCE**

Performance Expectations
ⅠⅠ TIME, CONTINUITY, AND CHANGE
   b. Apply key concepts such as time, chronology, causality, change, conflict, and complexity to explain, analyze, and show connections among patterns of historical change and continuity.

ⅥⅠ POWER, AUTHORITY, AND GOVERNANCE
   h. Explain and apply ideas, theories, and modes of inquiry drawn from political science to the examination of persistent issues and social problems.

Language Arts Skills
Reading, visually representing, speaking

Materials
- One copy of *The Power of One: Daisy Bates and the Little Rock Nine* by Judith Bloom Fradin and Dennis Brindell Fradin
- Sheets of butcher block paper
- Markers

Procedures
Allow students opportunities to read *The Power of One: Daisy Bates and the Little Rock Nine* or provide them with multiple copies. Have students respond to questions such as:
- Who was Daisy Bates?
- What was life like for African Americans when she was growing up?
- What social problems were occurring during this time?
- What is segregation and how did it affect Daisy and other African Americans?
- What kinds of conflicts were taking place because of segregation?
- Why did Daisy hate white people?

Read the words of Daisy's adoptive father. "Hate can destroy you, Daisy. Don't hate white people just because they're white. Hate the humiliations we live under in the South. Hate the discrimination that eats away at every black man and woman. Hate the insults. And then try to do something about it, or your hate won't spell a thing." (Fradin and Fradin 2004, p. 32-33).

Ask students to consider what Daisy did in reaction to her adoptive father's words. Divide students into small groups (4 or 5 per group) and give each group markers and a long sheet of butcher block paper. Have students create a chronology or timeline of the events in Daisy's life that occurred in reaction to her adoptive father's words. Students can use the book or other library or Internet resources to find out more about the events of the time.

Post completed timelines in the classroom and give each group an opportunity to discuss the events and experiences they included. Ask students to discuss the following questions:

- ▶ What caused Daisy to move from hatred to action?
- ▶ What brought about segregated schools and why was it so difficult to integrate them?
- ▶ What role did Daisy have in the integration of schools in Little Rock?
- ▶ Did Daisy have power and influence? If so, in what way?
- ▶ How did Daisy change from an ordinary citizen to someone of influence and status? What risks were involved?
- ▶ What does it take to bring about social change?
- ▶ Are all public schools integrated today? Why or why not?

Have students use library or Internet resources to investigate the status of integration in today's schools. Discuss the reasons for resegregation and why change is so difficult.

BODY BIOGRAPHIES: REPRESENTING HISTORICAL FIGURES THROUGH ART AND WRITING

***Linda Brown, You Are Not Alone: The* Brown v. Board of Education *Decision*, edited by Joyce Carol Thomas. (New York: Hyperion, 2003).**
Genre: A compilation of non-fiction, poetry, and autobiography

Book Summary

This is an edited book of stories, poems, and personal reflections from children's authors who lived at the time of the *Brown v. Board of Education* decision. Their writings tell the story of Linda Brown and what she meant to this country. The authors also tell of personal experiences in their schools and communities in 1954, related to issues of racism and segregation. Writers who are familiar to middle and high school grade students, such as Jean Craighead George, Lois Lowery, and Jerry Spinelli, share their collective experiences on a topic that continues to affect our lives today.

Social Studies Standards
🄊 **TIME, CONTINUITY, AND CHANGE**
🄌 **CIVIC IDEALS AND PRACTICES**

Performance Expectations
🄊 **TIME, CONTINUITY, AND CHANGE**
  e. Investigate, interpret, and analyze multiple historical and contemporary viewpoints within and across cultures related to important events, recurring dilemmas, and persistent issues, while employing empathy, skepticism, and critical judgment.
🄌 **CIVIC IDEALS AND PRACTICES**
  e. Analyze and evaluate the influence of various forms of citizen action on public policy.

Language Arts Skills
Reading, speaking, visually representing, writing

Materials
- ▶ Multiple copies of *Linda Brown, You Are Not Alone: The Brown v. Board of Education Decision* edited by Joyce Carol Thomas
- ▶ Butcher paper
- ▶ Markers, paints, colored pencils
- ▶ Library and Internet resources

Procedures
Introduce the *Brown v. Board of Education* decision and discuss its history. Explain the role of Linda Brown and her family in that court case, and discuss the impact of segregation and desegregation on our nation's history. You may choose to read aloud the introductory chapter "Who is Linda Brown" by Joyce Carol Thomas.

Have students read the remainder of the book. Involve students in a discussion of questions such as:
- ▶ How did Linda Brown and others make a difference in the promotion of desegregation?
- ▶ What qualities did these citizens share?
- ▶ How did the role of children in desegregation differ from the role of adults?
- ▶ How would you describe the reactions to the *Brown v. Board of Education* decision?
- ▶ What themes are present in the stories told by these authors?

Divide students into small groups. Have each group construct a body biography of Linda Brown by first drawing her silhouette on butcher paper. Ask students to represent within the silhouette Linda's life, experiences, and personality characteristics. Students are to use words, pictures, and drawings in their representation. They might also respond to themes in the stories, such as racism and segregation. Students can use symbols and colors to reflect the history and mood of the period. They can consider where in the silhouette they might wish to represent Linda's goals, feelings, and impact on United States history. Students can be encouraged to write poems, reflections, or interview responses to be included in the silhouette. Encourage students to seek additional information on Linda Brown and the desegregation of public schools through library and Internet resources.[1]

Give each group an opportunity to share their silhouette; explain symbols, colors, pictures, drawings, and design; and read the poems and reflections.

In the large group, ask students to consider the following:

- ► Have issues of racism and desegregation been resolved? Explain.
- ► What is the current status of segregation in our public schools?
- ► Why wasn't a federal law enough to rid the country of segregation?
- ► What can citizens do to continue to make change in segregated practices and attitudes?

Note

1. Modified from Amy Jones. "Body Biography," In Joan Elliott and Mary Dupuis, *Young Adult Literature in the Classroom: Reading It, Teaching It, Loving It* (Newark, DE: International Reading Association, 2002).

STUDENTS' OPINIONS ON WOMEN IN SPORTS: CREATING A HUMAN BAR GRAPH

A History of Basketball for Girls and Women: From Bloomers to Big Leagues by Joanne Lannin. (Minneapolis, MN: Lerner Publishing, 2000).

Genre: Nonfiction

Book Summary

Basketball was invented in 1891 by James Naismith, so that boys at the YMCA in Springfield, Massachusetts, would have something to play between baseball and football seasons. The original game used peach baskets for hoops, with a ladder close by so the ball could be retrieved after each basket. Within days, girls at the YMCA were playing it, and within a month, Senda Berenson had modified it for her female students at Smith College. A group of female teachers also became interested in the game when they happened to pass by the YMCA. They were considered the "New Women" of the 1890s, being born during a time when women were fighting for their rights.

The rules for women's basketball were different from those for men. The game was not quite as rough, and women wore long dresses or bloomers. In those days, many doctors believed that physical activity might harm a women's health and reproductive capabilities. The game quickly spread across the country, and basketball stars such as Babe Didrikson, Hazel Walker, and Stella Waterman gained notoriety. However, it was not until Title IX was passed in 1972 that women were able to earn college basketball scholarships.

In the 1976 Olympics, the United States had their first women's basketball team, which beat Czechoslovakia to win the silver medal. Concerns were present in women's basketball in the 1970s, including racism and homophobia. However, the game continued to gain momentum, and the Women's Professional Basketball League was formed. Women earned paltry salaries of $8,000 - $12,000 per season, and the WBL eventually folded. High school and college teams continued to prosper in the 1980s, and teams spent more money on women's sports programs in order to comply with Title IX. Female coaches filed lawsuits to earn equal salaries, and the struggle for equality continued even into the 1990s. The women's team earned their third straight gold medal in the 1992 Olympics, but were housed in the Olympic village, while the men's team stayed in luxury hotels.

Social Studies Standards
- **TIME, CONTINUITY, AND CHANGE**
- **CIVIC IDEALS AND PRACTICES**

Performance Expectations
- **TIME, CONTINUITY, AND CHANGE**
  b. Apply key concepts such as time, chronology, causality, change, conflict, and complexity to explain, analyze, and show connections among patterns of historical change and continuity.
- **CIVIC IDEALS AND PRACTICES**
  e. Analyze and evaluate the influence of various forms of citizen action on public policy.

Language Arts Skills
Reading, listening, speaking, visually representing

Materials
- ▶ Multiple copies of *A History of Basketball for Girls and Women: From Bloomers to Big Leagues* by Joanne Lannin
- ▶ Masking tape

Procedures
As a pre-reading activity, give students the five-question women's basketball quiz. Ask students to share their answers and discuss each question.

WOMEN'S BASKETBALL QUIZ
- ▶ In what year did women first play basketball? (1891)
- ▶ What did women wear to play basketball during those early years? (Dresses or bloomers)
- ▶ What occurred in the 1970s that finally allowed women to earn college basketball scholarships? (Passage of Title IX)
- ▶ How did the United States women's basketball team perform during their first Olympics? (Won a silver medal)
- ▶ Name one famous women's basketball player.

Creating a Human Bar Graph

Sports Participation Statements
- ▶ Female coaches should earn the same pay as male coaches.
- ▶ Girls should have the same high school sports teams as boys.
- ▶ Girls should be allowed to play on boys' high school sports teams when a girls' team is not available.
- ▶ Girls should be allowed to wrestle on a boys' high school team.
- ▶ Boys should be allowed to play on girls' sports teams when a boys' team is not available.
- ▶ Boys should support girls' sports teams through game attendance, just as girls support boys' teams.
- ▶ Girls and boys should have an equal opportunity for college sports scholarships.
- ▶ Girls' and women's sports teams would not be where they are today without the passage of Title IX.
- ▶ Boys should be encouraged to participate on cheerleading squads.
- ▶ Girls' and boys' high school sports teams should have equal funding.
- ▶ Girls' and boys' high school, college, and professional sports teams should have equal media coverage.
- ▶ Title IX continues to have a positive influence on men's and women's sports.
- ▶ There is now equality in men's and women's sports at the high school, college, and professional level.

Have students read *A History of Basketball for Girls and Women: From Bloomers to Big Leagues*. Involve them in a discussion of the following questions:

- ▶ How has the game of basketball changed from the 1890s to the present?
- ▶ What concerns did some doctors and educators have about women's involvement in sports?
- ▶ How did the historical and political forces of various historical periods affect women's basketball?
- ▶ How did the fight for women's rights affect women's basketball?
- ▶ How have the actions of women affected equality in salaries, scholarships, and sports opportunities?
- ▶ What is Title IX, and what has it done for women's sports?
- ▶ How did racism and homophobia affect women's basketball in the 1970s?
- ▶ What do you think are the biggest concerns in women's sports today? How do those concerns compare with the concerns of the past? How do those concerns compare with the concerns in men's sports?
- ▶ Do you believe the author presented an unbiased view of the history of women's basketball? Why or why not?

Place a piece of masking tape on the floor in the front of the room, stretching from one side of the room to the other. Ask students to participate in the formation of a human bar graph on the topic of sports participation. The right side of the tape will represent "agree," the middle section of the tape "neutral," and the left side of the tape "disagree." When you read each statement, students will walk to the section of the tape that represents their opinion on that statement. Students in each section will form a line perpendicular to the line of tape, creating a human graph. Encourage students to make their own decisions on each statement, so as not to be influenced by their peers. After the graph is formed for each statement, ask students to turn to someone standing near them in their own section and discuss their feelings on that statement. Give students two to three minutes for discussion. Then have students turn to someone in line in another section of the graph, so they can compare and contrast their views. At this point, if any student wishes to change their opinion and move to another section of the graph, they may do so. Randomly call on students in various sections of the graph, and ask them to share their feelings on that particular statement. Remind students that there are no right or wrong answers, and that everyone should have a right to express their opinions. Continue to have students reform the graph with the remaining statements.

THE WOMEN OF 9/11: QUOTABLE QUOTES

Women at Ground Zero: Stories of Courage and Compassion **by Susan Hagen and Mary Carouba. (New York: Pearson, 2002).**

Genre: Nonfiction

Book Summary

This book tells the stories of 30 women who were considered heroes on September 11, 2001. On that day, they were firefighters, police officers, paramedics, and emergency medical technicians, all involved in efforts to save the lives of citizens in the Twin Towers. The perspectives of these women are unique, and their stories, learned through interviews, tell of their experiences that day as wives, workers, friends, and daughters. The authors also include the stories of three women who lost their lives trying to save others, told by family and friends.

Many of these women entered the scene at the Twin Towers voluntarily, while others were ordered to enter. One such example is Mercedes Rivera, a 23-year-old emergency medical technician. Rivera and her partner heard of the tragedy on their radio. As they were heading toward the scene, they saw the second plane fly into the South Tower. Rivera stood under a walkway so she wouldn't be hit by falling debris and people. She and other EMT workers were ordered to enter the World Trade Center by their captain. She describes the incredible fear and panic she and others experienced as they tried to help hundreds of people escape. She left the building to set up triage in another area and was in her ambulance when the buildings collapsed. Rivera thought she and her partner would be overcome by smoke and debris, and this is how she remembered those moments: "I curled up. I waited for those windows to blow. I waited for the ambulance to turn over. I waited for death. Once again, I said my blessings. I said, 'Jesus Christ, please let my parents know I love them.'"

This book offers a first-hand perspective of what people experienced that day. It is not easy to read about the horrors, but it is vital for young adults to know what happened. The book should be offered as optional, but not mandatory, reading.

Social Studies Standards

Ⓥ INDIVIDUAL DEVELOPMENT AND IDENTITY
Ⓧ CIVIC IDEALS AND PRACTICES

Performance Expectations

Ⓥ INDIVIDUAL DEVELOPMENT AND IDENTITY

g. Compare and evaluate the impact of stereotyping, conformity, acts of altruism, and other behaviors on individuals and groups.

Ⓧ CIVIC IDEALS AND PRACTICES

b. Identify, analyze, interpret, and evaluate sources and examples of citizens' rights and responsibilities.

Language Arts Skills

Reading, listening, speaking, writing

Materials

▶ Multiple copies of *Women at Ground Zero: Stories of Courage and Compassion* by Susan Hagen and Mary Carouba
▶ Books of quotes
▶ Internet access

Procedures

Discuss the events of September 11, 2001, and have students brainstorm about all those who aided in recovery efforts. Introduce *Women at Ground Zero*, and advise students that it is a difficult book to read. Invite those who are interested to read select interviews of the women who were involved in recovery efforts. Even those who do not read the interviews can participate in a discussion of the following questions:

▶ How would you describe the women who helped with recovery on 9-11?
▶ Do you think EMT workers should have been ordered to enter the Twin Towers? Why or why not?
▶ How do you think these women developed unselfish attitudes and courageous personalities?
▶ Many of these women described the fear they had, but it did not prevent them from helping. Why do you think this was the case?
▶ What responsibilities would you say average citizens had, if they were in the area of the Twin Towers on that day? Explain.

Ask students to find two quotes that could describe the attitudes, personalities, and behaviors of the women who participated in rescue and recovery on 9/11. They can research books of quotes, such as *The Change-Your-Life Quote Book* by Allen Klein,[1] *Quotable Quotes* by Reader's Digest,[2] and *1001 Motivational Quotes for Success* by Thomas Vilord;[3] or access www.poemhunter.com and click on "quotations." After each student has selected two quotes, have students write the reasons why those quotes best describe the women of 9/11, using evidence from the text. In small groups, have students share the quotes they selected and the ways they represent these women.

Have students compile their quotes and make a bulletin board to honor the women of 9/11. Encourage students to discuss design and illustrations and to include a memorial to the three women who died.

Notes

1. Allen Klein. *The Change-Your-Life Quote Book* (New York: Gramercy, 2000).
2. Reader's Digest. *Quotable Quotes* (1997).
3. Thomas Vilord. *1001 Motivational Quotes for Success* (Cherry Hill, NJ: Garden State Publishing, 2002).

ADDITIONAL YOUNG ADULT AND ADULT LITERATURE TITLES FOR THE HIGH SCHOOL GRADES

Maya Angelou. *I Know Why the Caged Bird Sings* (New York: Bantam, 1969).

In this autobiography, Maya Angelou tells the stories of her youth. Her disappointments and frustrations are recounted, such as being sent to live with her grandmother and having an unwanted pregnancy.

Barbara Brackman. *Civil War Women: Their Quilts, Their Roles, Activities for Reenactors* (Concord, CA: C & T Publishing, 2000).

This book includes profiles of nine women of the Civil War era. Quilt designs of the time, activities for reenactors, and hands-on projects supplement historical information.

JoAnn Chartier. *With Great Hope: Women of the California Gold Rush* (Guilford, CT: Falcon, 2000).

This volume contains the stories of twelve women who experienced the gold rush. Tales of gold rush banking, cannibalism, lost love, and fortune make this book an interesting read.

Linda Scott Derosier. *Creeker: A Woman's Journey* (Lexington, KY: University Press of Kentucky, 2002).

This memoir tells the story of one woman and her life in the Appalachian Mountains of eastern Kentucky. She describes the close-knit community she grew up in, the days spent gardening and visiting neighbors, and the complexity of the Appalachian culture.

L. M. Elliott. *Annie, Between the States* (New York: HarperCollins, 2004).

This novel recounts the story of Annie, who lives in Virginia during the Civil War. Virginia fluctuates between North and South control, and Annie's brother fights for the north while her younger brother becomes involved in a vigilante group.

Webb Garrison. *Amazing Women of the Civil War: Fascinating Stories of Women Who Made a Difference* (Nashville, TN: Rutledge Hill Press, 1999).

Fascinating women, such as Harriet Tubman, Mary Walker, and Belle Boyd, are highlighted in this volume. From slaves to spies to surgeons, this book provides insight and interesting illustrations.

Joan Marie Johnson (Ed.). *Southern Women at Vassar: The Poppenheim Family Letters, 1882-1916* (Columbia, SC: University of South Carolina Press, 2002).

Sisters May and Louisa Poppenheim left their prominent Charleston, South Carolina home to attend Vassar in the 1880s. Their letters home chronicle the challenges they faced, such as their mother's desire for them to remain proper Southern ladies, while they desired to become activists for women's rights.

Laurence Learner. *The Kennedy Women: The Saga of an American Family* (New York: Ballantine Books, 1996).

Five generations of Kennedy women are chronicled in this volume of cultural history. This book carries readers from immigrant ships and the slums of Boston to the White House.

Judy Barrett Litoff (Ed.). *Since You Went Away: World War II Letters from American Women on the Home Front* (Lawrence, KS: University Press of Kansas, 1995).

This book offers a portrait of the United States during World War II, based on letters women wrote from the home front. The author uses 25,000 letters to portray the hardships, work experiences, shortages, and pain that families experienced while men were at war.

Karen Surina Mulford. *Trailblazers: Twenty Amazing Western Women* (Flagstaff, AZ: Northland Publishing, 2001).

This book features the lives of 20 great women who grew up out west or traveled to the west. The awesome feats and adversities of women such as Sacagawea, Sandra Day O'Connor, and Georgia O'Keefe are highlighted.

Martha Rhynes. *Gwendolyn Brooks: Poet from Chicago* (Greensboro, NC: Morgan Reynolds Publishing, 2004).

This biography tells the life story of award-winning poet, Gwendolyn Brooks. Brooks views on social integration and racial pride are reflected throughout this volume and many of her poems are included.

Ann Rinaldi. *Taking Liberty: The Story of Oney Judge, George Washington's Runaway Slave* (New York: Simon Pulse, 2004).

In this novel, Oney Judge is a favorite servant to Martha Washington. Oney learns to read and lives a good life with fine clothes. Excerpts from primary source material, including George Washington's writings, are included.

Harriet Sigerman. *Elizabeth Cady Stanton: The Right is Ours* (New York: Oxford University Press, 2001).

This biography tells the story of one of the most important women's rights activists of the nineteenth century. The author includes quotes from personal letters and Stanton's memoir.

James Alexander Thom. *Follow the River* (New York: Ballantine, 1981).

This novel is based on the true story of Mary Ingles, who, at age 23 and pregnant, was captured by the Shawnee. Mary escaped and traveled over one thousand miles through untamed wilderness to return to her family in Virginia.

CHAPTER 6

Conclusion and Recommendations

High-quality history instruction prepares students for civic responsibilities and involvement in democratic practices. In general, history has been taught from a male perspective, with little attention to the contributions of women.[1] In fact, women have been largely invisible in history classrooms, in part, because very few women are portrayed in history textbooks. Although recent studies indicate some progress is being made toward gender balance,[2] history textbooks continue to include significantly more males than females.

History instruction that relies on textbook-based instructional approaches has been described as dull and boring, with memorization of names, dates, and places as standard fare. In such classrooms, students lack skills in historical problem-solving and interpreting the past, and teachers lose focus on best practices.[3] This dissatisfaction, coupled with time constraints and the mandates of the No Child Left Behind Act, have led many teachers to consider the benefits of integrating history with the language arts. Literature for children and young adults acts as a bridge between history and the language arts, and is considered by some to the most effective means of teaching history.[4] Trade books foster readability through more complex sentence structure, longer sentence length, and incorporation of story elements such as plot, setting, character, theme, and point of view.[5] High-quality literature also brings a human element to historical studies, cultivating interest and engagement.[6]

Many children begin school with a body of acquired historical knowledge. Although young children do not fully understand historical chronology, they do understand the basic concept of time, and can differentiate past and present.[7] Informal history instruction should begin in the primary grades, so students have a framework for the formal teaching of history that typically begins in the intermediate grades.[8] One challenge in primary grade history instruction is assuring that methods are developmentally appropriate. Picture books are an excellent resource for teachers striving for developmentally appropriate materials and strategies, and many books with strong female protagonists are available. Children can employ visual literacy skills by viewing and analyzing illustrations, increasing opportunities for historical understanding.

By the intermediate grades, students begin to differentiate

historical periods and are able to associate dates with events in history.[9] Levels of understanding are developmental, and students in grades four through six continue to benefit from primary sources such as maps, diaries, photographs, and artifacts. Teachers can utilize both chapter books and picture books, with the latter providing the visual cues many students need for comprehension of story elements, time period, people, and events.[10]

In the middle and high school grades, students benefit from diversity in reading materials and book choices. With Internet access, adolescents can investigate accuracy and credibility of sources, just as historians do. Small-group work is essential, as students need opportunities to discuss, debate, and participate in consensus building.[11] At this level, students are able to use hypothetical reasoning to detect bias and consider the political impact of historical events. Students use critical literacy to interpret historical knowledge. They identify the winners and losers of history, explore big ideas (such as prejudice), and analyze perspectives that are included and voices that are silenced.[12]

Recommendations

As teachers move away from traditional, textbook-based approaches to history instruction, they begin to integrate literature, primary sources, and artifacts as bridges to the past. Such methods, although viewed as the most effective means of teaching history, can also be complex and labor intensive. The recommendations that follow are designed to assist teachers as they make the transition to literature-based history instruction and the integration of women's history into the classroom.

Use textbooks as a classroom resource. Although history instruction should not be dependent on textbooks, they do offer a concise overview of important events and people in history. While literature brings drama, depth, and varying perspectives to historical understanding, textbook references allow students to connect those understandings with other events during a given time period. Therefore, textbooks, Internet sources, and reference materials should be available for student use as they are reading and interpreting high-quality literature. Since few women are present in history textbooks, students can also benefit from analyses and discussions of textbook bias, treatment of women, patriarchal perspectives, and famous women who have been omitted.

Consider the benefits of integrating history and the language arts. This is especially advantageous in the elementary grades, where time is always an issue and teachers are accountable for student progress in reading and writing. Teachers can use historical literature from a variety of genres to teach reading and other language arts skills, so history is no longer an add-on to an already busy day. In the middle and high school grades, teachers of English and history can team-teach, sharing both instruction and assessment of student projects. For example, in one school, after students read books about the Holocaust, they submit a written paper to their English teacher and a project of their choice to their history teacher.

Begin history instruction early, in the primary grades. Informal instruction, integrated with language arts, provides students with basic historical understandings and a concept of time. Then students are better prepared when formal history instruction begins in the intermediate grades. Teachers should always strive for developmentally appropriate teaching methods, so young children view history as active, fun, and interesting. There are now an abundance of picture books with strong, interesting, and adventurous female characters. Including these books in classroom libraries affords students the opportunity to read them during independent reading time.

Be selective when choosing literature. Just because a book is about a woman in history does not necessarily mean it is a book you should share with students. When making book selections, consider readability, factual accuracy, bias-free text, visual appeal, multicultural diversity, and historical significance. Also ensure there is variety in genre, with a mix of historical fiction, biography, poetry, and nonfiction. Give special consideration to books that have received recognition, such as winners of Caldecott and Newbery Awards, the Coretta Scott King Award, the Parents' Choice Award, and the Michael L. Printz Award granted by the American Library Association. National Council for the Social Studies also selects Notable Social Studies Trade Books for Young People every year based on high literary quality. In addition, when making selections, don't limit use of picture books to the primary grades. Simple text and illustrations bring historical understanding to many students who are not able to comprehend more difficult chapter books. There are also some picture books whose content is not developmentally appropriate for young children, making them more suitable for the intermediate grades and beyond.

Focus on historical understanding and disciplined inquiry. The big ideas and human element of history are what students need to remember, and not necessarily the names, dates, and places. Encourage students to explore history as historians do by asking questions and examining the historical significance of events. Stress relevance by allowing students to investigate the relationship between the past, the present, and their own lives.

Assess students' misconceptions about history, and confront and correct them. Students often have many misconceptions about history, including women's history. Encourage them to use a variety of resources to examine misconceptions, stereotypes, and the accuracy and credibility of sources.

Make women's history fun and interesting for both boys and girls. Incorporate hands-on, active approaches to instruction and use artifacts and primary sources. Boys tend to enjoy adventure, biography, and information books, so providing them with choices, rather than assigning books, will help to maintain their interest. Allow students to explore some of the little-known women in history, and those who took tremendous risks to further their cause. Before sharing a book with the whole class, build background by discussing the author, time period, and events of the era and their historical significance. Challenge gender stereotypes and routinely share books with strong female characters, thereby reducing the "gender tension" that is often present when students are making reading selections.[13] Consistently expose boys to books about women in history, and they will become more comfortable crossing gender lines when choosing books to read.

Use a team approach to planning and design of curriculum materials. Work closely with grade-level or subject-area teachers to choose literature, develop historical themes, and plan instructional strategies. Dividing the curriculum development responsibilities among several teachers makes the process of integrating women's history into the classroom feasible for everyone. Also, the extension activities in this bulletin can be easily redesigned for different book selections. Teachers can determine what objectives they want students to master, or which of the six language arts skills they wish to emphasize, when choosing or creating extension activities.

Differentiate instruction when possible. Most classrooms now have great diversity in students' skill levels. Therefore, it is imperative to incorporate the literature and extension activities in this bulletin in ways that will benefit all students. When giving students the opportunity to make literature choices, ensure that books with a wide range of reading levels are available. Students tend to choose books with a comfortable reading level. When classroom copies of trade books are available and everyone is reading the same selection, allow students choices in how they will read each book. Some students will read the book independently, others may read with a buddy, and a few may need to read in a small group with direct instruction from the teacher. Also, remember that students enjoy listening to books read aloud, even in the middle and high school grades. This method affords even students with word recognition difficulties the opportunity to comprehend more difficult literature. Extension activities may need modifications to meet the needs of gifted students or those with special needs. For example, instead of writing a letter, those students who exhibit difficulties with written expression may choose to dictate their letter into a tape recorder. In addition, simply providing students with choices in extension activities, focusing on all six of the language arts, assists in meeting individual student needs and maintaining interest.

The children's literature to which students are exposed holds the beliefs and values we as a society have about gender. Literature on women in history has the potential to affirm or broaden students' perspectives on gender and the role of women in shaping our nation. When teachers select books that entice students to become engrossed in stories, identify with characters, and learn women's history, they challenge gender stereotypes and bring balance to the teaching of history. 🖋

Notes

1. L. Reese, "Report on Gender Equity and History Texts at the Secondary School Level," *Transformations* 5 (1994): 62.

2. R. Clark, "How Much is the Sky? Women in American High School History Textbooks from the 1960s, 1980s, and 1990s," *Social Education* 68 (2004): 57-62; Kay Chick, "Gender Balance in Current K-12 American History Textbooks," *Social Studies Research and Practice* 1 (2006): 284-290.

3. Gary Fertig, "Teaching Elementary Students How to Interpret the Past," *The Social Studies* 96 (2005): 2-7; Yali Zhao and John D. Hoge, "What Elementary Students and Teachers Say about Social Studies," *The Social Studies* 96 (2005): 216-222.

4. K. Nawrot, "Making Connections with Historical Fiction," *The Clearing House* 69 (1996): 343-345; Kay Chick, "Historical Nonfiction and Biography in the English Classroom: Bridging the Past and the Present," *SIGNAL Journal* 30 (2006): 11-15.

5. D. Richgels, and C. Tomlinson, "Comparison of Elementary Students' History Textbooks and Trade Books," *Journal of Educational Research* 86 (1993): 161-171.

6. C. Finn and D. Ravitch, "No Trivial Pursuit," *Phi Delta Kappan* 69 (1988): 559-564.

7. Keith Barton and Linda Levstik, "Back When God Was Around and Everything": Elementary Children's Understanding of Historical Time," *American Educational Research Journal* 33 (1996): 419-447.

8. Bruce VanSledright and Jere Brophy, "Storytelling, Imagination, and Fanciful Elaboration in Children's Historical Reconstructions," *American Educational Research Journal* 29 (1992): 837-859.

9. Stephen Thornton and Ronald Vukelich, "Effects of Children's Understanding of Time Concepts on Historical Understanding," *Theory and Research in Social Education* 16 (1988): 69-82.

10. Barton and Levstik, 419.

11. G. Wells and G. L. Chang-Wells, *Constructing Knowledge Together: Classrooms as Centers of Inquiry and Literacy* (Portsmouth, NH: Heinemann, 1992).

12. Steven Wolk, "Teaching for Critical Literacy in Social Studies," *The Social Studies* (2003): 101.

13. E. Dutro, "But That's a Girl's Book! Exploring Gender Boundaries in Children's Reading Practices," *Reading Teacher* 55 (2001/2002): 376-384.

Books Reviewed in Depth

The following books were discussed in detail in Chapters 2-5. Books are listed in the order in which they were discussed.

Author	Book Title(s)	Genre	Grade Level	Standards*	Extension Activity
David Adler	*A Picture Book of Sojourner Truth*	Biography	Primary	2, 10	Open-Minded Portrait
Shana Corey	*You Forgot Your Skirt, Amelia Bloomer*	Biography	Primary	2, 10	Flannel Board
Leslie Connor	*Miss Bridie Chose a Shovel*	Historical Fiction	Primary	1, 2	Emigrating to America
Kathleen Krull	*A Woman for President: The Story of Victoria Woodhull*	Biography	Primary	2, 10	How many is 100?
Emily Arnold McCully	*Marvelous Mattie: How Margaret E. Knight Became an Inventor*	Biography	Primary	2, 8	Invention Design
Deborah Hopkinson	*Girl Wonder: A Baseball Story in Nine Innings*	Historical Fiction	Primary	2, 6, 10	Artifact Prediction
Don Brown	*Alice Ramsey's Grand Adventure*	Biography	Primary	2, 8	Timeline
Alexandra Wallner	*Grandma Moses*	Biography	Primary	2	Five Senses Poem
David Adler	*A Picture Book of Rosa Parks*	Biography	Primary	2, 10	Commemorative Coins
Pamela Duncan Edwards	*The Bus Ride that Changed History: The Story of Rosa Parks*				
Robert Coles	*The Story of Ruby Bridges*	Biography	Primary	2, 4, 10	Character Analysis
Sandra Day O'Connor	*Chico*	Autobiography	Primary	5, 6	Dinner and Conversation

*   The NCSS Standards references are to the ten themes of the NCSS social
     studies standards. For convenience, all ten themes are listed on the inside
     flap of the back cover of this book.

Author	Book Title(s)	Genre	Grade Level	Standards	Extension Activity
Karen Winnick	*Sybil's Night Ride*	Biography, Historical Fiction	Intermediate	2, 4	Semantic Character Analysis
Trinka Hakes Noble	*The Scarlet Stockings Spy*				
Anne Rockwell	*They Called Her Molly Pitcher*	Biography	Intermediate	10	Story Pyramid
Jane Kurtz	*Bicycle Madness*	Historical Fiction	Intermediate	2, 10	Student Contracts
Nikki Grimes	*Talkin' About Bessie: The Story of Aviator Elizabeth Coleman*	Biography	Intermediate	2, 6	Readers' Theater
Sue Stauffacher	*Bessie Smith and the Night Riders*	Historical Fiction	Intermediate	2, 10	Newscast from the Past
Elizabeth MacLeod	*Helen Keller: A Determined Life*	Biography	Intermediate	4, 10	Anticipation/Reaction Guides
Marissa Moss	*Rose's Journal: The Story of a Girl in the Great Depression*	Historical Fiction	Intermediate	2, 3	Journal Writing
Gare Thompson	*Who Was Eleanor Roosevelt?*	Biography	Intermediate	10	First Lady Advertising Posters
Ann Whitford Paul	*All By Herself: 14 Girls Who Made a Difference*	Poetry	Intermediate	2, 6	ABC Lists
Cheryl Harness	*Rabble Rousers: 20 Women Who Made a Difference*	Biography	Intermediate	2, 10	Women's History Quilt
Lynne Cheney	*A is for Abigail: An Almanac of Amazing American Women*	Biography	Intermediate	2, 10	Alphabet Books
Pat Derby	*Away to the Goldfields*	Historical Fiction	Middle School	7, 8	Top Ten Lists
Ann Rinaldi	*Girl in Blue*	Historical Fiction	Middle School	6, 10	Historical Fiction Collages
Seymour Reit	*Behind Rebel Lines*	Biography	Middle School	4, 10	Literature Report Cards
Karen Hesse	*Witness*	Historical Fiction	Middle School	2, 4	Artifact Book Reports

Author	Book Title(s)	Genre	Grade Level	Standards	Extension Activity
Judith Bloom Fradin and Dennis Brindell Fradin	*Jane Addams: Champion of Democracy*	Biography	Middle School	6, 10	Snapshot Biographies
Dennis Brindell Fradin and Judith Bloom Fradin	*Fight On! Mary Church Terrell's Battle for Integration*	Biography	Middle School	2, 4, 10	Sentence Stem Scramble
Russell Freedman	*The Voice that Challenged a Nation: Marian Anderson and the Struggle for Equal Rights*	Biography	Middle School	2, 10	Book Detectives
Penny Colman	*Rosie the Riveter: Women Working on the Home Front in World War II*	Information, Nonfiction	Middle School	2, 7	Data Charts
Karen Hesse	*Aleutian Sparrow*	Historical Fiction	Middle School	1, 6	Venn Diagrams
Pam Nelson, Dawn Chipman, Mari Florence and Naomi Wax	*Cool Women: The Thinking Girl's Guide to the Hippest Women in History*	Biography, Fiction	Middle School	2, 6	Biopoems
Penny Colman	*Girls: A History of Growing Up Female in America*	Nonfiction, Biography	Middle School	2, 6, 10	Community-Based Research
Cokie Roberts	*Founding Mothers: The Women Who Raised Our Nation*	Biography	High School	2, 10	Research Discussions
Kathleen Thompson and Hilary Mac Austin	*The Face of Our Past: Images of Black Women from Colonial America to the Present*	Pictorial Nonfiction	High School	10	Interior Monologues
Ann Rinaldi	*Hang a Thousand Trees with Ribbons: The Story of Phillis Wheatley*	Historical Fiction	High School	2	Poetry Analysis and Illustration
Suzanne Jurmain	*Forbidden Schoolhouse: The True and Dramatic Story of Prudence Crandall*	Biography	High School	2, 6, 10	Send-A-Problem
Ann Rinaldi	*Numbering the Bones*	Historical Fiction	High School	2	Writing Epilogues

Author	Book Title(s)	Genre	Grade Level	Standards	Extension Activity
Mary Jane Auch	*Ashes of Roses*	Historical Fiction	High School	2, 10	Read a Book in an Hour, Action Planning
Donald Wigal Candace Fleming	*The Wisdom of Eleanor Roosevelt* *Our Eleanor: A Scrapbook Look at Eleanor Roosevelt's Remarkable Life*	Nonfiction, Biography	High School	4, 10	Quotation Analysis, Powerpoint Presentations
Judith Bloom Fradin and Dennis Brindell Fradin	*The Power of One: Daisy Bates and the Little Rock Nine*	Biography	High School	2, 6	Timeline
Joyce Carol Thomas	*Linda Brown: You Are Not Alone: The Brown v. Board of Education Decision*	Nonfiction, Poetry, Autobiography	High School	2, 10	Body Biographies
Joanne Lannin	*A History of Basketball for Girls and Women: From Bloomers to Big Leagues*	Nonfiction	High School	2, 10	Human Bar Graph
Susan Hagen and Mary Carouba	*Women at Ground Zero: Stories of Courage and Compassion*	Nonfiction	High School	4, 10	Quote Selection, Bulletin Board Design

About the author

Kay A. Chick is an Associate Professor of Curriculum and Instruction at Penn State Altoona. She holds undergraduate degrees in elementary and special education, graduate degrees in educational psychology and school psychology, and a doctorate in curriculum and instruction. Before her move to Penn State Altoona in 1998, Kay was a special education teacher and school psychologist. Her research interests include gender issues in education, social studies, and children's literature. She currently teaches courses in educational theory and policy and educational psychology to elementary and secondary education majors. Kay has co-authored two other books, *Multicultural American History Through Children's Literature*, published by Teacher Ideas Press in 2003, and *Activities for Standards-Based, Integrated Language Arts Instruction*, published by Holcomb Hathaway in 2007.

Kay lives with her husband, Bill, in Indiana, PA, with their younger son, Tim, and their dog, Christopher. Kay and Bill's older son, Tyler, is finishing up his last year in college. They enjoy bike riding, hiking, and travel.

This index includes the titles of books listed and annotated at the end of chapters, as well as books discussed in detail in the chapters.

Author Index

This index includes the authors of books listed and annotated at the end of chapters, as well as books discussed in detail in the chapters.

M

N

O

P

Q

R